RETREAT
FROM
REVOLUTION

RETREAT
FROM
REVOLUTION

THE DÁIL COURTS, 1920–24

Mary Kotsonouris

With a Foreword by Brian Farrell

IRISH ACADEMIC PRESS

First published in 1994 by
Irish Academic Press
10 George's Street
Newbridge
Co. Kildare
Ireland
www.iap.ie

9781788551250 (Paper)
9781788551267 (Kindle)
9781788551274 (Epub)
9781788551281 (PDF)

British Library Cataloguing in Publication Data
An entry can be found on request

Library of Congress Cataloging in Publication Data
An entry can be found on request

Typeset in Minion Pro 11.5/15 pt

Cover artwork: 'Republican Court' by Seán Keating
© Estate of Seán Keating, IVARO Dublin, 2020.
Image photography courtesy of David Yelverton.

This book is dedicated to the memory of the accused, the plaintiffs and defendants, the witnesses, officials, registrars and clerks, the justices and judges, the victims, supporters and critics of the Dáil Éireann Courts.

And with their memory is coupled the memory of three men whose absence was keenly felt all through the years of research – my father, Johnny Raleigh of Limerick, William Binchy, lawyer, and Donal Foley, newspaperman.

Contents

Foreword

The story of the 'Irish revolution' in the early twentieth century has always been problematic. Despite Yeats's rhetorical flourish, a terrible beauty was not born. The Irish Free State in many ways reflected a political system largely in place before the Easter Rising of 1916. The promise of major social and economic change spelled out in the Democratic Programme of the First Dáil remained a dead document as Ireland settled down to run its own affairs. The constructive work of the old Sinn Féin parliament in the Mansion House was forgotten.

Yet this early Dáil was a vital bridge between the old Ireland and the new. Had circumstances, and personnel, been different, its consequences might have been far more radical. Sinn Féin set out in 1919 to create 'a polity within a polity'. Nowhere was it more successful than in the creation of an alternative administration of justice.

This important and persuasive monograph is the first comprehensive account of the court system set up by the First Dáil. Too often a monograph is described as a 'forgotten page' of history; the implication is that it merely deals with a detail that does not significantly alter the accepted version of past events. *Retreat from Revolution* deals with no mere footnote in modern Irish history. It offers a critical and revealing key that should unlock a new understanding of the origins and development of the new Irish state.

It uncovers, for the first time, the detailed story of how Ireland turned its back on an established network of Sinn Féin courts and opted to adopt a legal system remarkably close to the status quo. The rigmarole of wigs and gowns was only the outward manifestation of the innate conservatism of the legal and political establishment of the Irish Free State. Mary Kotsonouris is ideally placed to chronicle this remarkable and complex story. Her training as a historian and her experience as a judge give her a unique insight and indisputable authority in weaving her way through documentation that has been far too long neglected. Out of these archival riches she has fashioned an intriguing, important and eminently readable reconstruction of a seminal phase in Irish historical, legal and political development.

The author summarises this remarkable book in the first sentence of the introduction:

> The story of the courts established by the First Dáil is both simple and extraordinary: simple in its concept, extraordinary in its execution and its effects.

The reader will reflect that the comment aptly applies to Mary Kotsonouris's achievement in *Retreat from Revolution*.

Brian Farrell

Preface to the First Edition

W hat began as mere curiosity on my part about the Dáil Courts, and a sense of there being an inherent contradiction in the idea of subversive courts, was fuelled by the discovery of a treasure trove of documents with the records of the Dáil Courts Winding-up Commission in the Public Record Office at the Four Courts. The type of proceedings, the complaints of the litigants and the delay in the execution of judgements were instantly familiar to a person working in the administration of law. Having taken the narrower field of the Commission itself as the subject of research for an M.Litt. thesis, I was determined to write a book for the general reader about the Dáil Courts and their importance in the lives of the people who used them. The book is based on contemporary records and newspaper reports; the opinions expressed, unless otherwise attributed, are wholly my own.

The Dáil Courts were extraordinary courts that operated in an ordinary way and paralleled in their proceedings and procedures those of the courts they were intended to subvert. They were the promise and the proof that the time for self-government had come. Later, when the Civil War meant the temporary shelving of civil liberties, judicial independence was perceived as something ominous, so the courts were abruptly suppressed. I tend to the view that the subsequent denigration of the courts by the authorities sprang from a sense of shame over the undemocratic way in which they had suppressed them. In later years, when the emphasis on the armed struggle came to eclipse the quieter revolution based on civil disobedience, the courts tended to be dismissed as ineffective, or a, or unimportant. No evidence was adduced to show that they were all or any of those things at the same time. What we do know is that the people who used the courts were no more critical of them than their descendants are of the present legal system. It is only in a perfect world that a losing party would never criticise a court!

Scholars have, of course, written about the Dáil Courts: in particular, I have found the articles in the *Irish Jurist* by James Casey and Brian Farrell very illuminating. Judge Conor Maguire gave the keynote address on the subject some years ago at the Merriman Summer School: his father, and namesake, the later Chief Justice, had been a Dáil Land Judge and wrote about his experiences in *The Capuchin Annual*. I have reason, as many more gifted than I have had, to be grateful to the late Leon O'Broin for his advice.

I could not have written this book without the active help of a great number of people. I have no words adequately to describe that given to me by the staff of the National Archives, the Gilbert Library, the National Library, Trinity College Library, the Military Archives and Seamus Helferty of the Archives, University College, Dublin. Everyone took time and trouble to answer even the most casual enquiry. I am also grateful to the directors of all these institutions for allowing me to quote from the documents in their keeping.

Professors Brian Farrell and Nial Osborough have always been ready to fill in the very large gaps in my knowledge. Maurice Moynihan, a former Government Secretary, and Judge Gerard Burke of Galway, who was a registrar in the Dáil Circuit Court, received me in their homes and answered my avalanche of questions with unhurried courtesy: it is a source of pride to me to count them as friends. I was also fortunate to be able to speak to the children of those who feature in these pages and I thank them for their patience: Mrs Moira Gillespie, daughter of Mr Justice Creed Meredith, Mrs Ann McDonagh and Lorcan Heron, whose mother was a judge of the Rathmines District Court, Cahir Davitt, and Aidan and the late Donal Browne, sons of Dan Browne, as well as many other people who told me of family connections with the courts or local lore about them. I am particularly grateful to the family of the late Mr Justice Davitt and to Kevin Haugh S.C. for having been given access to an unpublished memoir (in Mr Haugh's possession) containing a first-hand account of the operation of the courts in which Judge Davitt played such a central role. I am equally grateful to Mr Colm Gavan Duffy, who loaned me unpublished papers belonging to his late father. Dr Tony Varley of University College, Galway, was kind enough to let me read a paper he had given in Belfast on agrarian crime and the Sinn Féin courts, and to send on a copy of its subsequent publication. Mr Justice Ronan Keane and Charles Lysaght, both legal historians, have generously allowed me to read drafts of books soon to be published. As an untrained newcomer, I have been overwhelmed by the generosity of real scholars, particularly by Professor Brian Farrell's kindness in writing the foreword.

The Arthur Cox Foundation, which has done so much to support the publication of legal books in Ireland, has kindly come to the aid of this book; I am most grateful for its help.

I am indebted to Dr Curt Adler for his helpful comments on the text and his assistance in preparing the manuscript for typing. I thank my friends Maeve Binchy and Gordon Snell for their unfailing support and encouragement and also Aodhan O'Higgins, Jonathan Williams, James White, Thomas Ryan, Peter Murray of the Crawford Museum and Art Gallery, and Michael Adams. Lastly, for many reasons, there is a special appreciation to be expressed to my children, Vassily and Anna Kotsonouris.

Introduction

The story of the courts established by the First Dáil is both simple and extraordinary: simple in its concept, extraordinary in its execution and its effects. The well-spring of the hope that disputes might be amicably settled is universal in civilisation and dies at the first breath of legal precedent and the pursuit of self-interest. Arthur Griffith thought that in the Utopian society which would flower when the Irish governed themselves, arbitration courts, freed from the grasp of time-serving lawyers, would resolve otherwise contentious issues with justice, goodwill and dispatch. Although he put forward the proposal as early as 1905 at the National Convention, and returned to the theme in 1912 and again in 1919, it is unlikely that he gave much consideration to the more gritty problem of how law and order were to be administered, much less how an arbitrator's finding was to be enforced if one side reneged. After the 1918 election, abstention from Westminster, which at different times since the Act of Union had been considered as a tactic by O'Connell, Parnell and Redmond, was now the stated policy of victorious Sinn Féin to be put into effect. The seceding MPs became TDs in Dáil Éireann which met for the first time at the Mansion House, Dublin, on 21 January 1919. However, it was the Democratic Programme, largely the contribution of the Labour Party, and not the Sinn Féin Constitution, which was introduced as the statement of social and economic policy: there was no reference to the administration of justice. The impetus to change the legal system came from another direction.

The outbreak of serious agrarian violence in the west of Ireland spread like a contagion. There was a recklessness abroad that warned local leaders of the danger threatening the renewed pride in national identity and the hope of independence. Small groups of influential men offered their services as mediators, and this encouraged disputants to bring all kinds of grievances to 'Sinn Féin Courts' as they rapidly came to be called. At the same time, the Volunteers took it upon themselves to act, not only as the local constabulary, but to hold trials and administer punishment. Both developments greatly contributed to alienating public consciousness from the established court system, and within a very short time a network of alternative tribunals was being used for the adjudication of various quarrels, through a combination of persuasion, fear and the attraction of novelty. Dáil Éireann, which had taken few steps to implement its decree of August 1919 that arbitration courts were to be established on a national scale, was forced into taking a lead when its Agriculture Minister was persuaded to appoint a judge to hear a dispute about land in Mayo, and inevitably, to call on the IRA to enforce the court's decision when it was flouted. Although Austin Stack, the Minister for Home Affairs, had begun to promulgate an official scheme for arbitration, the Dáil was finally moved to initiate its own hierarchy of civil and criminal courts by June 1920. They served to build regulated structures on foundations laid by the people themselves, a fact that may have escaped the attention of their elected representatives, who in any case, because of their own precarious existence, had little contact with what today would be called the grassroot level. The parochial courts did have, however, but the politicians could not bring themselves to acknowledge the fact when calmer times came and they were able to assert their authority.

The trouble was they saw success as a matter of prestige, of self-congratulation and shining proof that the Irish were capable of governing themselves. The effectiveness of the Dáil Courts was all that, but it was of much more importance to the thousands of people who used them to resolve their disputes, assert their ownership, divorce their spouses. They had, long before the Treaty, invested in ultimate nationalist victory by deserting the courts rightly considered the brightest jewel in the British tradition, whose decisions would be enforced by the Crown, and had taken their legal proceedings to various shabby halls, or outhouses, or rooms above shops to be decided by men – and sometimes women – as unremarkable as themselves. Some commentators have tended to dismiss the courts as a bit of Irish drollery to rival Somerville and Ross. It is not difficult to highlight the case about the trespassing pig who ate the cabbages, or the goose won in a card game who kept returning to her previous owner. However, it is unlikely that there is anyone working in the District Court today who would not at least attempt to cap those cases with others of more recent experience. Not everyone needs reminding by Patrick Kavanagh of the epic nature of many a local row. However, all that is to ignore the long procession of prosaic actions for debt, non-performance of contract, breach of warranty and other civil suits of interest only to the parties themselves. It is unlikely that commercial firms would have wasted resources in litigation in these courts, particularly against one another had they not been persuaded that the exercise was worthwhile. To give only one example: a long-drawn out refusal by tenants of the Dublin Artisan Dwelling Company to pay an increase in rent had already been heard in the High Court. While the tenants were collecting money for an appeal to the House of Lords, it was the landlords who first approached the Dáil Ministry with a request for arbitration.

The truce gave the Dáil Courts the opportunity to entrench themselves in the civil and commercial life of those living outside Northern Ireland so that, when the Treaty was signed, no move was made to displace them. In fact, special care was taken to allay widespread anxiety on that point, in spite of the contrary Proclamation of the Provisional Government. To save face, the courts were maintained under the ostensible direction of the Dáil Ministry. No attempt was made to curtail their jurisdiction or to rehabilitate the statutory courts that had been all but obliterated. It is impossible to guess how long they might have held their ascendancy if civil war had not broken out. It was not Judge Crowley issuing a habeas corpus order for a political prisoner that sparked the closure of the courts and the only revocation of a Dáil Éireann decree, as is widely believed: it was the judge's defiance of an executive direction suspending his judicial function that threw the Provisional Government into a panic. The decision to close the courts had already been taken two weeks previously and ignominiously announced in the Supreme Court within three days. However, even a month before, definite if tentative steps had been taken to revive the Assizes; and, since it is impossible to conceive that persons charged with a crime were going to be given a choice, not only of their mode of trial, but of jurisdiction also, the move can be interpreted only as the beginning of the end. That poses yet another question – why bother, when the draft Constitution embodying a new legal system had already been approved at the time? Speculation here is a Pandora's Box and leads to quests that have proven fruitless. It is not a shortage of records: there is a wealth of documentation for this period in public records in Ireland and in England, but the reasons given for what was obviously a considered political decision constitute hollow propaganda, patently at odds with the facts.

The mystery is more intriguing than the truth, wherever that may lie. It is not merely the secrecy and the cryptic memoranda that hedged it about, but the hysteria, the paranoia and the petty persecution that was vented for a very short time on those judges and officials who expressed the democratic view that it was for parliament to decide such matters, not the executive. What rankles, however, is the abandonment of the people, who had been persuaded, coaxed or herded into these idealised courts in their thousands. One searches the records in vain for some recognition of the loss and bewilderment of individuals, or the betrayal of those who had risked life and liberty to serve the Dáil judicial system, absolute loyalty to which had been collectively decreed by those now in power. Not quite in vain, though, because George Gavan Duffy resigned in protest and Henry O'Friel, Secretary of the Department of Justice, led the effort to establish a judicial commission which had the effect of re-installing the Dáil Courts in some pomp and circumstance, ensured that their jurisdiction merged with that of the new High Court – and ended costing the Irish Free State far more than it would have if the Provisional Government had paused long enough to consider its chairman's question before deciding to bring its most blazoned creation – the courts of Dáil Éireann – crashing down. It was Michael Collins who wondered if there were any courts that the people could go to instead.

The immediate answer to that problem was the appointment of twenty-seven District Justices (the title chosen in an effort to blur any connection with Resident Magistrates, because appointed under of the same Act as had created that office), who were sent out into the country at the beginning of November 1922, without structures, rules, and – in many cases – without courthouses. They were, for the most part, young lawyers who had to make out as best they could, bringing the rule of law to a civil population still reeling from one war while being plunged into another. It could scarcely have been foreseen that they would be left on a jurisdictional limb for almost two years to serve as a signpost that the administration of law had passed into native hands. The story of the District Court and its impact on the newly independent rural Ireland awaits its Hampden. Within a year the Judicial Commission to process the mountain of cases left unfinished in the Dáil Courts was set up, and while it was only beginning to make some headway, the Courts of Justice Act, which created the legal system for the Irish Free State, was passed in May 1924. The Bill had taken over eight months to go through the Oireachtas due to the steady and stubborn refusal of deputies and senators to allow any vestige of control over the judges to remain in the hands of the Executive. The District and Circuit Courts of the new dispensation were modelled on the Dáil Courts system: moreover, the corpus of judgements with the revived jurisdiction of the Dáil Courts were transferred the following year to the High Court and remain there to this day.

What did the Dáil Courts mean in the development of independent Ireland? The present writer is neither a historian nor a jurist, and certainly not that which might be of more relevance – a sociologist. While learned persons from these disciplines have written articles that illuminate different aspects, my task has been simpler; that is, to relate the story from the idea of operating alternative courts that paralleled those of the state to their eventual absorption into the legal system we have today. The main difficulty was in the wrench of discarding much that clamoured to be included, so dense are the records in the National Archives. I began reading these files when I was a judge in the District Court and consequently felt no sense of strangeness, much less of quaintness, in the subject matter. It is from that perspective that I write, in the hope that others, more qualified, will benefit from having something solid between covers. It may well be that perception of the place of the courts in communal life suffered because of the instant denigration, required by political expediency, which followed the *schluss* that closed them. It is fervently hoped that a new generation of scholars might now look beyond that and make all kinds of discoveries in a phenomenon that seems to have been unique in modern times. They might also find a fruitful field of study in tracing a possible connection with the general attitude of the Irish people towards their courts. They have a proper expectation of the highest standards, but they do not put judges on any kind of pedestal. Their interest in law is passionate and knowledgeable: they take it for granted that the judiciary is free of government control, and they criticise the whole process relentlessly.

1

The People's Courts

When Arthur Griffith addressed a convention in the Mansion House on 6 December 1905,[1] the programme that he outlined was part of an unstructured imagining of an ideal he had been pursuing through writing, talking and debate for over twenty years. His audience had come together under the umbrella of the National Council, whose original purpose was the uncomplicated one of opposing addresses of loyalty to the monarch. Among other sympathisers was the Sinn Féin League which fitted in comfortably with one of Griffith's teeming ideas, that of making Ireland self-sufficient in industry and agriculture. The various interests represented at the meeting recall Roy Foster's description of 'a radical avant-garde of cultural nationalism';[2] everyone was a separatist of one kind or another, although there were as many versions of that as there were schisms. None of these groups, however, was a political party; nor, at that time, aspired to be. Griffith was using his meetings and publications as a forcing house for ideas on independence, sovereignty and abstention and as a distancing from English culture, fashion and character.[3] Therefore, the proposal to establish national arbitration courts must be regarded, not as a policy, but as part of the vision of a new Ireland that was in a state of constant flux. There were many influences being brought to bear upon the core idea of repeal of the Union and a ferment of theories about nationhood, political economy, republicanism or dual monarchy. There is no evidence to suggest that any particular thought was given to what national arbitration courts would entail – whether they could be extended beyond the conciliation of civil disputes, as the term suggests, or if that limitation was intended merely to coincide with the adjunct scheme of commercial enterprise and self-sufficiency.

When one looks at the 1905 Convention and the agenda so airily sketched out, it can hardly be called a benchmark for the courts that evolved fifteen years later. Even as late as 1912 Sinn Féin was still a fragile alliance of disparate and heady disputants, but at least they had got down to writing a constitution, where the item about the courts clearly stated that their task would be 'the speedy and satisfactory adjustment of disputes'.[4] This was a worthy, if somewhat woolly, idea of formal arbitration, but certainly not a realistic concept of a proper civic court. One wonders at the optimism of 'satisfactory': it could hardly be that for the losing party.

When all had changed utterly after 1916 and Sinn Féin became the wide umbrella that sheltered so many unlikely comrades, it had also become a political party in the metamorphosis.[5] It fielded candidates for election and put together a constitutional programme that used the material to hand – ballot boxes and the locally elected councils – as a blueprint of a civil administration. It succeeded in setting up Arthur Griffith's great dream in January 1919 – a constituent assembly composed of elected MPs who had withdrawn from Westminster and sat as the parliament of Ireland, now called Dáil Éireann.[6] Ministers were appointed and Arthur Griffith was given the Home Affairs portfolio. It was very exciting and the response in the rise of nationalist sentiment is discernible in all quarters – municipal, ecclesiastical and sporting. To read a paper like the *Limerick Leader* right through 1919 and 1920 is to trace a prideful consciousness of national identity, supported by church and civic leaders, gradually becoming overwhelmed by coat-trailing and staged encounters between the police or military and young men anxious to test their mettle. Life became increasingly dangerous and descended swiftly into acts of brutality as 1919 drew to an end. The Defence of the Realm Act, usually referred to as DORA, was invoked to proclaim various districts under martial law, which caused resentment in the community because fairs and markets were disrupted. Public figures condemned the random shooting of local policemen, but were silent on the marching, drilling and possession of revolvers, for which increasing numbers of young men were imprisoned: in fact, the newspaper headings showed their disapproval with words like 'harsh' and 'drastic' to describe a twelve-month sentence.[7] On whom did the elders think the guns were going to be used except on policemen and soldiers?

It is difficult to understand in the light of the strong current rushing towards self-determination apparent in newspapers over these months that any person, other than the most bone-headed militarist, could have believed that this momentum could be turned around. However, the response to youths jeering at soldiers from a street corner in Limerick was to take up firing positions and kill a publican shutting up his shop and a cinema usherette returning home from work.[8] From the autumn of 1919 onwards the toll of these incidents is unremitting, and yet the paradox of the few arrests for what was, even then, being called 'ordinary crime' was frequently commented upon. Military tribunals and Crimes Courts constituted under the Defence of the Realm Act and Restoration of Order in Ireland Act 1920 dealt with the political violence,[9] while at the Assizes and Quarter Sessions the traditional white gloves piled up and the Petty Sessions sat for only minutes, such was the shortage of business. Lord Justice O'Connor, commenting on the absence of indictable cases at Limerick Assizes in the face of rising lawlessness, said 'whatever these gloves may fit, they do not fit the condition of the city'.[10]

In the midst of the ferment, it was to be expected that agrarian vandalism, reminiscent of the Whiteboys, would surface, as it had over and over again in the past hundred years. Where the leaders thrown up by the Sinn Féin movement had the moral authority, they were able to exercise it to impose a negotiated settlement and this was generally perceived as being fair to the landlord. While no doubt preferable to having his animals turned out to starve or his family and himself assaulted, it was, at the end of the day, a forced sale in many instances. It must be borne in mind, however, that a scheme of land acquisition was already in place with the Wyndham Act of 1903,[11] so that it could be argued – and was – that these arbitrations were being substituted for the inefficiency of the Congested Districts Board which had failed to release enough land to satisfy the demand. There can be no doubt that many claimants would have felt justified in taking possession without any recompense. Had they not been told by successive national leaders that they had been robbed of the land in the first place? The long-nurtured grievance and the long-expected deliverance spawned such a conditioned response that the arbitrators had difficulty in making one set of claimants understand that they were now, in fact, landowners themselves and could not claim as tenants. It was ironical that the particular claim was being made against Edward Martyn, the first President of Sinn Féin.[12]

Many areas in Munster, particularly in County Clare, were proclaimed under martial law because of cattle driving and general defiance of the law during 1919. In response to the same problem, ad hoc courts were first put in place. The leaders had every reason to fear that the old spectre of agrarian terrorism would rise again by using name of Sinn Féin as a convenient flag for any bully boy to terrify a farmer or torment his neighbour, if he had a mind to. It was set to undermine the increasing confidence in a nationalist programme, so ways of conciliation were sought to mediate the genuine grievances of landless men by setting up tribunals to adjudicate and fix a price in compensation and to decide who would be permitted to purchase the land. Moreover, here and there, groups of Volunteers began to act as village constables, restraining rowdyism and investigating larcenies. They also meted out the punishment, ordering that, in addition to returning property or making good the damage, the offender would be fined or banished to another county, or even marooned on an island for a period. There were other forms of punishment, less complicated and more immediate in their effect, which were described in press reports as 'drastic' or 'due punishment meted out' before the miscreant was released. It was an innovation that pleased the *soi-disant* law-abiding of the community – and was increasingly accepted by those who were on the receiving end of this rough justice. Two men who had disobeyed an order of a Sinn Féin tribunal to rebuild a wall they had demolished were left on an island off the Clare coast for three weeks. A party of the Royal Irish Constabulary who arrived by boat to rescue them were pelted with stones and abused. The castaways proudly declared that they were citizens of the Irish Republic and the police had no right to interfere.[13]

Newspapers such as the *Limerick Leader*, the *Tipperary People* and the *New Ross Journal* carried regular reports of Volunteers investigating and adjudicating in respect of assault, robbery and licensing offences during the first half of 1920. Under an eye-catching headline, 'Sinn Féin Justice', the *Freeman's Journal* gave a summary of the work of the Volunteer patrols in 21 counties over a six-week period. It was a strange mixture – dispelling a riotous assembly, imposing the licensing laws, swift retribution for property damage and larceny, protecting women from abusive language, as well as solving bank and post-office robberies. The paper admitted that the information had been supplied to it, and the attempt by the Sinn Féin publicists to harness the success of the Volunteers to its wagon was reflected elsewhere, particularly in the Westminster House of Commons, whose members saw most of the benighted Irish, including several southern unionists, besotted by Sinn Féin and its siren call to non-conformity. But even if propaganda, the details of dates and places given in the *Freeman's* report were impressive.[14] Of more dramatic impact was the story in another paper on the same day of a 'Sinn Féin Court' held at midnight in a Tipperary bog. It was, in fact, a court-martial, although the defendant was not a soldier: a Volunteer officer was assigned to defend John Ryan, charged with stealing mail bags and bicycles and beating his father, who had made the complaint. While the Volunteers had searched for him, they in return were being hunted by a 200-man force of police and military in the eastern part of the county. When Ryan was captured at three in the morning, he was supplied with a candle so that he could verify the warrant for his arrest. During the week he was detained, he was given good food and work spreading farm manure; he still managed to escape and hide in a farm-cart. When he was discovered, he called out in panic, 'For God's sake, don't shoot!' Among the items recovered were cheques and title deeds belonging to a local lawyer. The culprit was banished from the province of Munster for two years.[15]

The sentence imposed frequently took the form of banishment from the parish, locality or county for varying periods. As punishment, it had the advantage of being severe, inexpensive and primitive. There can be no doubting the deprivation it must have caused to young men without experience or resources, too terrified to disobey the order or to risk being betrayed by neighbours if they did. In more severe punishments, the guilty person was, like Columba, banished from Ireland, which caused a protest in the House of Commons on the numbers of undesirable people being deported to England and on the 'use of England as a sort of convict settlement for men deported by Sinn Féin'. It was felt that the Irish Attorney General did not intervene because it suited him to have such unsavoury persons out of his jurisdiction.[16]

The defiance of established law and order and the increasing reliance on an alternative discipline did not operate in isolation. There was a steady attrition of justices of the peace resigning their commissions. The reins of local government were largely in the hands of Sinn Féin supporters, and Poor Law Guardians increasingly looked to Dáil Éireann for direction.[17] While confrontation between the military and the public resulted often in the deaths of uninvolved citizens, the toll of local policemen shot in churches, in the streets or visiting their families mounted with sickening regularity. The local administration of justice was uninvolved with this frightening phenomenon: political crimes occupied the attention of courts martial or Crimes Courts: the scope of the normal courts had been radically curtailed. Sinn Féin tribunals or the vigilante-type Volunteers concerned themselves only with preserving the peace as traditionally understood and settling civil disputes; there was no attempt to claim jurisdiction over the activities of the Irish Republican Army. For much the same reason, white gloves continued to be handed to judges with a great deal of civic pride at official court commencements. A dangerous air of unreality is discernible among those not in the front-line – wherever that was located in the Ireland of 1920. There was a guerrilla war going on, unfocused in its targets, and the control of civil administration had been coolly alienated from central authority, yet it did not appear to impinge on the British government, which alone had the power to change the established order. Leaders of opinion at every level in England were pointing out, as Chesterton did, that 'Ireland was lost to England'. The *Daily Mail* said: 'An Irish Republic is very nearly in being' and censured the raids on the courts as childish. Lord Dunraven, an Irish unionist, wrote to *The Times*:

> An illegal Government has become the de facto Government. Its jurisdiction is recognised. It administers justice promptly and equably and we are in this curious dilemma that the civil administration of the country is carried on under a system the existence of which the de jure Government does not and cannot acknowledge and is carried on very well. The logical deduction is that profound dissatisfaction with the origin of the law, not with law and order, is the cause of the trouble.[18]

It was an accurate summary of a development that had deprived the British cabinet of taking refuge in the irradicable tendency of the Irish towards lawlessness, but it was a surprising analysis for a unionist, since the 'logical deduction' was that the law should originate in a changed structure. There must have been some to whom it was clear that, whether armed resistance intensified or not, real power had already shifted to men who would not easily relinquish it. Indeed, in July 1920 Alfred Cope, who was Assistant Under-Secretary in Dublin Castle, warned a cabinet conference in London that the Sinn Féin Courts were doing more harm to the prestige of the government than the assassinations.[19]

More importantly, did Dáil Éireann wonder if power was passing too rapidly to the people? It had failed to exercise any direct control over what had happened so far in these courts, which were spontaneous and localised. Individuals were referring all kinds of cases to them, including slander, trespass and rights of usufruct. Matters were withdrawn not only from the lower courts but from the High Court in Dublin: solicitors were faced with the bleak prospect of having to break stones for a living, as one of their number had forecast at the Strokestown Quarter Sessions.[20] The *ersatz* courts were becoming quite formalised in their procedure, issuing in junctions and summoning juries. The elected representatives of the people who were sitting as Dáil Éireann – or those of them who were still at liberty – had not taken any steps to exercise ostensible authority over these self-governing tribunals, nor made any provision for a legal regime to regulate their proceedings. Neither was there evidence of a general desire to see them brought under Dáil control.

Although the Dáil had decreed as early as August 1919 that a scheme of national arbitration courts was to be set up and a committee appointed to devise schemes to put the decree into effect, it was left to individual constituencies to make their own arrangements. The committee did not meet regularly, and progress in bringing forward a definite plan was slow.[21] West Clare was the only place where a constitution was drawn up and courts operated on parish and district levels.[22] In May 1920 Austin Stack,[23] the Minister for Home Affairs, was finally in a position to send out a circular which provided for three arbitrators to be elected by the parish and adjudicate on claims under £10. All parties were to undertake to abide by the decision of the court and to comply with its orders, subject to a right of appeal – an interesting refinement on the idea of submission to arbitration. The appeal lay to the District Court, which was presided over by five arbitrators who were elected by members of the parish courts. Their jurisdiction was unlimited. Remuneration was to be paid to the arbitrators between one and two pounds per day.[24]

There was an added impetus for the Dáil to become involved around this time. A deputation of Connacht landowners had called on Arthur Griffith asking that he use his authority to set up independent land courts. All of them, according to Kevin O'Shiel's account, had 'had their fields cleared, their cattle and sheep driven along the hard roads of Connacht for miles until they died of exhaustion and hunger and the value of all was disastrously diminished'.[25] In the spring of that year, agrarian anger was particularly acute since the hopes of small farmers were bitterly disappointed at the auctions of eleven-month letting; unbridled fury was vented on land, cattle and, frequently, on the ranchers'.[26] There was little hesitation in using a patriotic guise to claim solidarity in these acts, such as branding appropriate beasts with the initials 'S.F.' or 'I.R.' or hanging a tricolour on the lands that were seized. As ever, patriotism was at hand for scoundrels to take refuge in. O'Shiel, in his recollections in the *Irish Times*, relates the story of such a band intent on helping themselves, who marched to their purpose under the tricolour. On being told that Sinn Féin was against land seizures, they tore off the orange and white and continued under the green flag of the Ancient Order of Hibernians. It is not without relevance that the landowners who talked to Griffith had already appealed to the RIC, which had been unable to spare the time or men to deal with agrarian trouble.[27] Already the support of those who would ordinarily despise them was being wooed by the Sinn Féiners.

It was an enormous public relations coup for the Dáil. Here was a class, whose prop and stay had been the Royal Irish Constabulary, being forced to turn to men regarded as rebel agitators for help in their desperation. Moreover, help was given and proved to be effective within a relatively short time. Art O'Connor, substitute Minister for Agriculture (the real holder of the office being in gaol), was sent to the west to investigate the situation and he was joined there by Kevin O'Shiel, who was the young Northern barrister whom Griffith had consulted. Conor Maguire was a solicitor practising with his brother in Claremorris and he was very worried about a particular claim which was being pushed by intimidation and boycott: the land belonged to two larger landowners, although neither held more than sixty acres. They would agree only to submit a case to arbitrators outside the district. Hence Maguire urged his visitors to act as such, and so great was his power of persuasion, that they managed to secure telephoned permission from Griffith to do so.[28]

Maguire, a future Chief Justice, represented the smallholders, and when the owner's solicitor baulked at representing them in an illegal court, the parish priest put his canon law training at their disposal. Thus it came about that the first court under the direct authority of Dáil Éireann sat at Ballinrobe, Co. Mayo on 17 May 1920. The sitting was widely reported, with a particular air of pride, in the nationalist press.[29] It led directly to a development which Griffith had feared. Judgement was against the claimants and some of them put on a public show of of defiance. Kevin O'Shiel saw how others followed this example, when he was sent to hold more courts after he had been appointed as Dáil Land Commissioner. It was inevitable that such challenges to the growing respect for Dáil government had to be faced, and he consulted Arthur Griffith. An IRA unit under Tom Maguire[30] rounded up some of the younger rebels and detained them on an island in Lough Corrib. After a week there they were ready to agree to promise unequivocal obedience to the orders of the court. This was, of course, a further inroad on the idea of arbitration as it is universally understood; it proved that Griffith's fears were justified. It was the end of his dream of consensus, non-violence and civil disobedience.

Force had certainly been used to a greater or lesser extent by the Volunteer 'police' to see that decisions were observed, but this might have been excused as local zeal. Now, Dáil Éireann was being forced to accept the consequences of its pretensions. If it was the democratic government of the people, then it had to be prepared, like every other government, to use the coercion and sanction necessary to impose the collective will. Not only that, it would have to show that it intended to use such force without hesitation and nationwide. The administration of justice could no longer be left to local initiative and autonomy. It led, inevitably, to courts with a coercive jurisdiction being quickly organised on a national basis with a standard legal regime. Moreover, once the Dáil cabinet called upon the IRA, either directly or in its loose form of Republican Police, it was a recognition of a link that was being forged, perhaps reluctantly where the constitutionalists were concerned; it was to prove something of an irritant to the fighting men.[31]

The Dáil had assured responsibility for the actions of the military republicans. President de Valera, in the United States, said on 30 March 1920: 'From the Irish Volunteers we fashioned the Irish Republican Army to be the military arm of the Government. The army is, therefore, a regular State force, under the civil control of the elected representatives, and under organisation and a discipline imposed by these representatives, and under officers who hold their commissions under warrant from these representatives. The Government is, therefore, responsible for the actions of this army.'[32] The picture that he painted had little basis in reality. It saddled the Dáil with responsibility for everything the IRA did, yet it had not means to exercise any effective control. O'Shiel's account of events some months later shows that Griffith had to engage in some arm-twisting before Cathal Brugha would take steps to ensure that Dáil Éireann's putative army would enforce its edicts.

Cooperation was never to be easy: the Republican police remained torn between the Army Command and the Home Affairs Ministry through all the time that the courts of Dáil Éireann operated. When Griffith sent the neophyte O'Shiel to Cathal Brugha, Minister for Defence, to ask for IRA assistance in the impasse after Ballinrobe, Brugha heard him out in silence before saying with absolute finality that he had no time for courts, police or their ilk. Nothing should be allowed to deflect attention from the paramount importance of the war: the rest were refinments that could be considered once the enemy had been forced out.[33] The tension between what came to be seen as the two parts of the national struggle never eased and each thought the other had the secondary role. There was the macho contempt of the fighting men for the pen pushers and, even though he brilliantly played both roles, more than his characteristic gaucherie lay behind Collins's taunt to Austin Stack that his department (Home Affairs) 'was a joke'.[34] Underlying the remark was the obvious contrast between the charismatic and forceful personality of Collins and the figure of a dyspeptic pedant which Stack presented. Whether meant or not, the comment was simply untrue. The Home Affairs portfolio was the widest in the Dáil ministry and no deputy had been appointed to assist Stack. In addition, the records show that the other departments passed over to Home Affairs enquiries which might prove too much trouble to pursue, and they were always taken on. While it adds enormously to the information to be garnered from the files, it would have lessened the workload considerably had the letters been promptly returned to the various offices to which they had been addressed in the first place!

2

The Legal Regime
of the Republic

There was an apparent reluctance to grasp the opportunity presented by the willingness of the people to abandon the regular courts at every level and embrace an alternative access to justice. Only a month before the passing of the decree authorising the establishment of regular courts, Austin Stack had set the arbitration scheme afoot. An arbitration courts committee had been set up which presented recommendations and reports at intervals, and the Dáil Ministry approved a scheme for parish and district courts on 13 May 1920.[1] The double initiative does represent a tentative step in bringing the local enterprise under the control of the Dáil and accepting the responsibilities of presuming to govern. Erskine Childers gives a concise account of the official arbitration scheme, but offers no explanation for its rapid replacement, other than that the arbitration structures were necessarily experimental and incomplete.[2] It was time to vest the courts with power to compel attendance of witnesses and to enforce their decrees, as well as putting into place proper arrangements for criminal trials. Childers does not allude to the waste of time in replacing one operation so rapidly with another, particularly when the same defects had been obvious since the start of the year.

The explanation may be that Stack, whose appointment as Minister was officially confirmed by the Dáil cabinet on 16 January 1920, took up the task that would have fallen to him under the National Arbitration Courts decree of June 1919 had he been at liberty then, and went ahead with examining ways to put it into effect. Over the following months and further consultations, it became clear that the current situation called for more radical thinking – what Professor Casey has characterised as 'a more structured system of courts with coercive jurisdiction'.[3] Nevertheless, Decree No. 5, Session 1, which was passed a year later than the Decree No. 8, Session 4, was also concerned with the administration of justice, but there was less than six weeks separating their execution. The decree of 29 June provided for courts of Justice and Equity, and the Ministry was empowered 'when they [*sic*] think fit to establish courts having a criminal jurisdiction'. The text reads:

The Minister for Home Affairs moved:

1. That the establishment of Courts of Justice and Equity be decreed.
2. That the Ministry be empowered when they deem fit to establish Courts having Criminal Jurisdiction.

He explained that the Courts hitherto established were purely Arbitration Courts which depended on the consent of both parties. The country was in such a state at the present time that the people looked to the Republican Government for their law and equity and in a very short time they would have ousted the English Courts altogether. It was therefore necessary to take immediate steps to set up Courts throughout the country which would be competent to hear every class of case similar to the cases dealt with in English Courts of Petty Sessions and Courts of County Sessions and Assize so far as Civil Jurisdiction was concerned.

He therefore moved for the necessary authority to enable him to establish such Courts and confer the necessary Jurisdiction upon them.[4]

The person responsible for the drafting must have thought either that there was a proper distinction between courts of justice and those called criminal courts, or that there were necessarily two stages to the initiation. Whatever the reason, the form of words used was to be the basis two years later of the suggestion that the Minister for Home Affairs had not been given power to set up the courts which he did.[5] By that time, the Provisional Government was casting around wildly to justify their abrupt closure.

A committee of lawyers was hastily formed to advise the Minister and to draw up rules,[6] which were published under the subtitle 'Judiciary' and were so referred to thereafter. In view of the claim that was later made – in particular by Hugh Kennedy, Law Officer to the Provisional Government – the opening words of *The Judiciary* state: 'The Aire Um Gnothai Duitche [Minister for Home Affairs] having been authorised by Dáil Éireann to establish Courts of Law and Equity and Criminal Jurisdiction as part of the Government of the Irish Republic, hereby decrees that there be established …'[7]

It was to be argued that the courts were only provisionally established.[8] Whatever the merits of that argument, it must be observed that, while the subheading 'Provisional Constitution' occurs under the title, there is nothing in the body of the constitution which leaves it open to the interpretation that the courts themselves were intended to be provisional; for example, although there is a reference to the future enactment of a code of laws, it is not linked to any possible change in the constitution. Moreover, the judges of the Supreme and Circuit Courts were appointed for life and were to be removable only by a special decree of the Dáil for a stated reason which required a two-thirds majority – a similar provision still applies.[9]

The courts established in accordance with the constitution were a Supreme Court, a District Court in every parliamentary constituency and a local court in every Roman Catholic parish. The procedure in the District Court was to correspond to that of the County Courts and the Parish Courts to the Petty Sessions. The applicable law was that which existed on 21 January 1919, the first sitting of the Dáil. This had the practical advantage that the law was known and not liable to change since it could not be affected by English decisions or by any fresh legislation other than that of the Dáil. Brehon, Roman, French and other law codes could be cited, but not any legal text published in [Great] Britain, an inexplicable piece of mean-mindedness, which reflected little credit on eminent legal persons who were immured in the Common Law and English precedents.[10] It may have been a policy directive but it should have been opposed, if only on the obvious grounds that it was impractical. The novel element, judicially speaking, was the introduction of a circuit tier to the District Court. Each was to have three 'Circuit Sittings' a year which would be presided over by a professional judge and which would have unlimited jurisdiction both in civil and criminal cases.[11] Equity and title matters were reserved to the Circuit Judge, but otherwise the decision of the ordinary judges on the facts of a case were of the same weight as his. Equity cases were defined as those involving trusts, mortgages and proceedings relating to an infant. It also served as an appellate court. The Supreme Court had unlimited original jurisdiction in prerogative writs such as *certiorari, prohibition* and *habeas corpus*. It could reserve a case from any court to itself for hearing and could decide criminal or Land Commission matters on a case stated.

The District Court in its ordinary jurisdiction was concerned only with civil matters, such as claims between £10 and £100 in value, and in land disputes where the valuation was under £30. It could determine cases of a higher valuation, provided there was no question of law involved and where a court decided that there was no possible defence – a curious stipulation since it presupposes a preliminary finding from which it would be difficult to exclude interpretation of the law. Like the County Courts, they also heard landlord and tenant matters, Workmen's Compensation and appeals from Parish Courts. It was in these latter courts that the effectiveness and influence of the revolutionary courts were most constantly and fiercely judged by participants. Claims of less than £10, minor crime and offences and ejectments in low rent dwellings all came before the Parish Courts, which also took evidence and sent forward those accused of serious crime. There were three justices elected by a convention which was composed of representatives of Sinn Féin, the Volunteers, Trades Councils, and Cumann na mBan within the locality: the president of the court was more often than not the local Catholic curate, not the parish priest. In turn, the collective parish justices elected the five members of the District Court: they chose their own chairman, and three could form a quorum. They held a court only once a month as an ordinary sitting. As it turned out, when the circuit judge presided, his court lasted for several days.[12]

Although some district judges were solicitors, there was no qualification necessary for the lower courts and the vast majority were laymen. However, the judges of the higher courts had to be lawyers and all those appointed were barristers. James Creed Meredith was a distinguished scholar, a doctor of philosophy and was a King's Counsel. Arthur Clery was Professor of Law at University College, Dublin and a practising barrister: they were both appointed judges of the Supreme Court. The Constitution had firmly stated that the court 'shall consist of not less than three members' but they were, in fact, only two. Equally there were to be at least four Circuit judges, but only Cahir Davitt and Diarmuid Crowley were ever appointed, although, later on, certain barristers and solicitors were given temporary commissions when extra circuit sittings were needed. Cahir Davitt, who was the son of Michael Davitt, had been four years at the Bar. Diarmuid Crowley was considerable older than him and had been called to the Bar only in 1916 after he had retired as a Customs official. All four were appointed for life according to the Constitution and received £750 per annum paid monthly. Conor Maguire and Kevin O'Shiel were appointed judges of the Land Commission, Maguire having expressed his preference for this work when he was offered a circuit judgeship. Both sat on occasion in the other courts when there was a shortage of judges.[13] Although a final appeal lay to the Supreme Court from a decision of the Land Judges, this is not their story, which remains to be told. Their jurisdiction came under the Ministry for Agriculture and their records are with those of the Land Commission in the National Archives.

Cahir Davitt writes that he was approached by his close friend and former professor, Arthur Clery, in the Law Library in July 1920, who told him about the proposed courts and that he had Stack's authority to offer him a judgeship. It was a surprising choice, particularly to Davitt himself, who was only twenty-six, but it was a fortunate one. Cahir Davitt was resourceful, cool and very judicial – which is interesting, because from that time until he retired as President of the High Court in 1966, he never worked as anything else except a judge of one kind or another. He comments that the reason why 'men so junior and inexperienced as Crowley and myself' had been approached was that men of more standing had refused and, moreover, that that was the reason why only four out of the proposed seven appointments could be made. Given that the Bar Council had set its disapproving face against its members participating in the separatist courts, it is interesting, if idle, to speculate why the field was narrowed to barristers: after all, there were talented solicitors associated with the courts from the beginning: one has to think only of the towering figure of Seán Ó hUadhaigh who acted as a sort of unofficial Attorney General to Dáil Éireann.[14] The regulations specified only 'legally qualified' persons, but it was overwhelmingly to 'the corrupt Bar of Ireland'[15] castigated by Griffith when he first introduced the idea of breakaway courts, and which had replied in kind by anathematising them, that the Minister turned to recruit his professional judges. When backbenchers in the House of Commons had questioned the Attorney General on what steps were being taken against barristers and solicitors engaged in 'illegal and treasonable practices' by participating in Sinn Féin Courts, he replied that it was a matter for their professional bodies, the King's Inn and the Incorporated Law Society.[16] It could hardly have been coincidental that the matter was raised within a short time with both. The Law Society could see no impropriety in its members protecting their clients' interests by appearing for them in Arbitration Courts.[17] The Bar Council took an entirely different view and in June 1920 passed a resolution that it was professional misconduct for barristers to appear at such tribunals. Although considered unacceptable by some, it was not officially challenged until five months later when, in November, Tim Healy told a general meeting of members in the Law Library that the General Council was acting *ultra vires:* it had not been acting within its power in passing a resolution of professional misconduct. Only the benchers of the King's Inn who admitted a man to the Bar could decide on the question of his fitness to practise. The meeting adjourned because of a plea by S.C. Browne, the Father of the Bar, that no friction should be allowed to disturb 'the happy family' that they all were.[18] This peaceful solution left undisturbed the decision on professional misconduct, as well as the more interesting question of the powers of the Bar Council.

Davitt also confirms from first-hand experience the trauma suffered by the regular courts in the spring of that year. He was just beginning to make some progress on the Western circuit as a junior in the County and Assize Courts in Mayo, Galway and Offaly, when he found it all being taken away from him, as litigation was increasingly transferred to the republican Arbitration Courts. In spite of his name, he was never offered a brief, and so had not appeared in a Republican Court until he did so as judge. Cases in which he had already been briefed were quietly transferred to another forum and disposed of without his assistance. At the opening of the Swinford Sessions, Judge Charles Doyle sat with solicitors, counsel, court officials and police assembled before him – and no one else. As the list for the day was called over, solicitors rose in succession to advise the court that they had no instructions in the matter, or that the case had been settled, or that a client was not present.[19] 'Everyone knew that the cases had gone to another jurisdiction, but the Republican courts were never mentioned.' To make doubly sure, the Volunteers had commandeered all the approach roads to the courthouse, and the only person allowed to make his way to the court, after considerable difficulty, was a local publican to make a licensing application. He had apparently been permitted through the *cordon sanitaire* 'in the public interest'.

The experience of one young barrister losing the advantage he had painstakingly garnered would have been mirrored in every circuit except the north-east. It is not surprising that some of them baulked at the Bar Council categorising those of its members who accepted a brief in a Sinn Féin Court as being guilty of unprofessional conduct. One of their number, W.H. Brayden, in an article on the courts published at some distance in the *Journal of the American Law Association*, grumbled that the only barristers ever disbarred for professional misconduct, whom he knew of, had first been found guilty of an offence in a court of law.[20]

Had they not been successful in availing of the loophole, the results would have been dire for most provincial solicitors. Only those who could have comfortably managed without a court practice would not have been driven to 'breaking stones', as predicted by the Strokestown solicitor in the preceding chapter. The interests of members whom the Law Society served demanded that they would not be impeded in making a living by the imposition of principles, but it was a bizarre situation and the splenetic protests by members of the House of Commons were not only foreseeable but quite proper in the circumstances – which were nothing less than the usurpation of the legal system of the United Kingdom. After all, solicitors were officers of the court, a dignity they were previously in the habit of asserting, and for them to transfer their skills – and their cases – to non-statutory bodies, while at the same time carrying on practising within the legal framework at their *à la carte* convenience, could be explicable only in terms of the schizophrenic society that was being taken for granted on all sides, excepting a few backbenchers in the Commons. It was disingenuous to make the argument about arbitration.[21] These courts were brought into existence as part of a flagrant challenge to the established order and their increasing dominance was heavily underscored by the tactics of the Volunteers and the general non-cooperative attitude towards the other courts – even to refusing lodgings to the Assize judges.[22] While barristers may have been threatened with disbarment for appearing at Sinn Féin

courts, James Creed Meredith became the President of the Supreme
Court of the Irish Republic by reason of his being a King's Counsel and
therefore the more senior judge.[23]

    This, then, was the background to the launch of the Dáil Court system,
which tended to appear, and indeed was, the expected development from
all that had gone before. It made little difference in the short term to
those attending the existing tribunals: in fact, the spirit of conciliation
continued to be attempted by most of the local courts as long as they
operated. Not only did this reflect their origins, it was in great part
due to a natural desire to preserve peaceful relations within the smaller
community in so far as possible. In fact, the provincial papers did not
stop reporting the proceedings as 'Sinn Fein Arbitration Courts' even
after the Dáil decree. It had followed so hard upon the instructions for
the Arbitration Courts that arrangements were being put in train for the
first only before it was superseded by the second. The *Tipperary People*
reported the first sitting of the District Arbitration Court at Nenagh. It
listed the live adjudicators by name and said the parties had been asked
to submit to the jurisdiction of the court.[24] In the same week armed
police raided a court in Limerick, confiscated the papers and arrested two
judges, one of them the former Mayor, Stephen O'Mara.[25] One of the first
reports to use the term 'Dáil Court' appeared in the *Tipperary People* on
30 July 1920 and it was to the effect that the police had taken possession
of the Town Hall in Castlebar to prevent the court being held there. It is
unlikely that there was a connection between any change in the courts'
status and the raids, which at that time seemed to depend on the view
taken by the local inspector or head constable, rather than an overall
policy. They do show that the smokescreen of arbitration did not prevent
the disruption of the proceedings in several instances in mid-1920. It is
as difficult to discern the seam that grafted the Dáil Arbitration Courts
onto the ad hoc tribunals which necessity had impelled into existence as
it is to see that which joined the former to the Dáil Courts proper. A year
was to pass before their formal structure was in a position to usurp the
administration of justice in Ireland to an extent that exceeded anything
that Arthur Griffith had imagined.

3

In Dark and Evil Days

The number of ministries within the Dáil Éireann cabinet was quite small, and that of Home Affairs was concerned with other functions besides the responsibility for the courts and the Volunteer police. Emigration was forbidden without a special permit, and the correspondence reveals the lobbying that had to be undertaken in order to get permission for a young person to join a sibling in America who could afford to send the passage money.[1] Most of the persuasive letters came from the parish priest or the local deputy. The Belfast Boycott had to be closely monitored also, and information about breaches investigated.[2] Licences generally and the White Cross relief fund for prisoners' dependants came under the Ministry's remit, but by far the greatest part of its work was the organisation of the courts.[3]

It was work that Austin Stack[4] felt himself particularly competent to direct. He was a doctrinaire republican who had worked as a solicitor's clerk in Tralee. He had been arrested in 1916 immediately after the capture of Roger Casement near Banna Strand in the bungled attempt to bring in arms by the German warship, the *Aud*. Indeed, he was in prison more often than not between that time and long after the end of the Civil War, being among the last to be released. The desire to prove himself capable of catching up on his ministerial colleagues may have led him to plunge into the arbitration scheme shortly before the decree authorising coercive courts was passed. He tended to think that a tight organisation and detailed directives were all that were needed to make the courts bulge with litigation. He discounted the background of armed confrontations and the inexperience of bureaucratic disciplines in the men hastily thrown into the role of court clerks. They were expected to comply with procedures, schemes and regimens, regardless of the difficulties of putting the apparatus of legal proceedings together in the face of official suppression and retaliation.

The man revealed in the spate of letters and circulars under his name is self-important, bullying and pedantic. Stack gives little thought to the problems of those he is addressing, and there is a distinct note, if not of hostility, certainly of suspicion.[5] He could be manipulative in distinguishing the courts which were able to continue through the worst of the Black and Tan times, but he rushed to answer criticisms, particularly those of Collins, who felt free to interfere in everyone's department. The contrast between them is striking, even in the tone of letters, but if Stack lacked the other's imagination and style, he had a proper sense of judicial independence and sharply pursued complaints of interference by IRA personnel. He was more in the mould of civil servant than politician: unfortunately, he was to have only a short time to be either. He followed de Valera like his shadow out of the Dáil and into the Civil War, and thereafter to prison and an uncompromising rejection of the reality of the Free State. When his leader abandoned that policy, formed the Fianna Fail party and went into the Dáil, Stack ceased to have a political future. A few years before, he had married the widow of an RIC inspector and began to study for the Bar. On the brink of domestic happiness and a new career, he died suddenly in 1929.

Patrick Sheehan was the first Secretary under Stack, but he was in prison over much of the period. Dan Browne acted as his substitute and his reference is at the head of much of the correspondence: he was a young solicitor from Tralee and was recruited by Stack particularly to work in the Courts Section. Certainly, when the organisation was invigorated about the time of the Truce, Browne was very much in charge of the revised system that was put in place. He remained a pivotal figure during the difficult period after the Treaty, as long as he was satisfied that there would be no dilution in the policy of supporting the native courts. He sensed a change of attitude in March 1922, months before it was evident to the others, and he resigned, to the consternation of Eamonn Duggan, his then Minister. After the Civil War, he returned to Tralee and established a successful practice as a solicitor when he was again summoned to Dublin. It was 1932 and de Valera was particularly worried about the status of the support his new cabinet might receive from the sensitive Department of Justice, as the Home Affairs Ministry had become. His trust in Browne was such that he considered him to be the most effective person to be Secretary of the Department should there be conflicting loyalties in the transition period. His fears proved illusory, and two years later Stephen Roche was appointed to replace Browne, who was made an appeals judge in the Land Commission and never returned to his practice in Tralee.[6]

It is ironic to reflect that after Stack's departure from the Ministry in January 1922, Browne had been at the centre of a similar conflict. Additional staff members were almost press-ganged into the Dáil Courts Section to be a counterweight to those who were already in place and who were perceived as being potential dissidents.[7] This development will be discussed later. T.V. Cleary, who had been dismissed from the established court service when he was suspected of being involved in the Rising and subsequently reinstated, acted as Registrar of the Supreme Court. He was to be dismissed again for being disloyal, according to the Provisional Government, but survived to serve for many years as the Chief Clerk of the District Court.

The secretarial work was done by Madge Clifford,[8] Kathleen Bulfin and Nora Brick. The task of getting the scheme off the ground, however, rested on the paid organisers, who numbered about ten men, stationed in different parts of the country. They arranged the conventions at which justices were elected and imparted the instructions to clerks and registrars on their duties. Local deputies and prominent Sinn Féin supporters were canvassed for information and the organisers acted as the eyes and ears of Stack on the ground and were treated as such. Some of their reports, which are with the records, show the network of influential men to which the organisers had access, as well as an insight into conditions in the area at the time.[9] The Ministry also had the benefit of shrewd comments made in letters written by the local deputy or the Volunteer commander. Not merely were the staff to be instructed in the manner of operating the courts and keeping proper records: enthusiasm for the work, belief in its success and defiance in the face of martial law also fell to the lot of the organiser to inspire amongst those he addressed at meetings. The local Sinn Féin club was central to the early organisation and to rallying support for the courts as Griffith had urged.[10]

Once the courts were established, their operation was the responsibility of the District Registrar in each parliamentary constituency. He arranged the sittings of the District Court, both in its ordinary and circuit

manifestations, issued the proceedings according to the instructions of
the applicants, as well as supervised the Parish Courts and filing reports
to the Ministry. An elaborate scale of fees served to fund the courts. A
party making a claim had to pay a deposit of 5 per cent of the first £100
in value and thereafter 2 per cent, up to a maximum of £10. Any party
appealing to the Circuit sitting was obliged to pay the same amount again
as had been paid on the original civil bill. This sum was not returnable,
being analogous to stamp duty, but might be added to the costs awarded to
a successful claimant. Where a complaint was made in a criminal matter
to the parish court, a sum of 3s. 6d. was payable, if the complainant was
not a Volunteer officer. There was a 6d. per mile extra where the person
against whom the complaint was being made lived more than two miles
distance from the court. The extra fee was to cover the cost of service
of the summons by the court messenger, but since the location of the
court was never to be certain until after the Treaty, such fees would have
been difficult to calculate. If the complainant was a Volunteer officer or
a member of the Republican police, then he was responsible for having
the summons signed by a Parish Judge and for seeing that it was served.
In other cases, this duty fell to the parish clerk. If the Court were to
find the defendant guilty of a criminal offence, it could bind him or
her over, impose a prison sentence, or order the payment of a fine and
compensation not exceeding £100. A fee of five shillings was payable
in a civil claim under £5, ten shillings if it were over. An appeal from
the decision of the Parish Court in any matter, civil or criminal, cost a
flat ten shillings. Although the rules (*The Judiciary*) did not refer to the
Republican Police, in Rule 16 there is a reference to 'a prosecution by the
State', a strange concept when it is remembered that these were drafted as
early as August 1920.[11]

The reports and the financial returns – either the lack or the
infrequency of them – were the subject of an endless stream of corrective
correspondence from headquarters, which insisted that its own rigid
and unreal demands be met.[12] The overriding impression is that there
was no pleasing the Minister. Even where his instructions were strictly
followed, he found grounds to complain. The ruling was that the District
Justices were to decide the weekly salary to be paid to the Registrar, and
the Parish Justices likewise for their clerks, yet no matter what sum, high
or low, was deducted from whatever court revenue was being forwarded,

there was almost invariably a furious rebuke, followed, most illogically, by the reiteration of its being the judges' decision to fix the amount of payment or, sometimes, that the Minister was not going to sanction it. Every penny that was spent from revenue was begrudged. There were sharp protests if a successful plaintiff was given back his deposit or a Republican policeman was paid for executing a warrant. The Parish Courts enjoyed more autonomy, principally because it was too difficult for the Ministry to establish a chain of command with them. It was a matter for the Registrar to control them and all he could do was give assurances that he had pointed out the correct procedure and was sure there would be no repetition of similar largesse.

Only idealism – and perhaps the hope of some future employment in whatever new state emerged – can explain why the registrars put up with being treated as if they were lazy, stupid and somewhat dishonest.[13] Their work was dangerous, difficult and diffused: most of the time they were not paid and many of them had other employment; and, of course, they provided a bone of contention for disappointed litigants. That they were educated men is evident from their letters: they were also resourceful and committed. In fact, in most instances, only those who were arrested, killed or called up for military duties by the IRA were replaced. It was ungenerous that their work was rarely appreciated by those who should have been in the best position to do so. There is little recognition in the correspondence that the Ministry, the organisers and the registrars, as well as the clerks, were all on the same side.

Reports began to appear of public meetings to set up what were still referred to as National Arbitration Courts throughout July 1920. The confusion did not lie only with journalists. It is clear from the remarks made by some participants that they thought that they were giving effect to the scheme launched by Stack in May. The *New Ross Journal* carried an account of such a meeting on 2 July, where the members of the court were appointed and a Father Harper spoke at considerable length about Arthur Griffith's dream of arbitration courts – which he had preached 'in season and out' for sixteen years.[14] At this very early stage there was considerable tolerance on a quasi official level. Several approving references to their success were made at Petty Sessions, as well as praise from Unionists because their lands had been freed of trespassers or their stolen property recovered and returned. Major Herries Crosbie, the Resident Magistrate for New Ross, publicly recognised that 'these courts which have been set up by the people are acting with the very best intention of keeping order in the country', although that did not absolve him from the duties he had been appointed to carry out.[15] The provincial papers in July and August carried a steady stream of reports of Parish Courts being set up all over and gave the names of the justices appointed, as well as full accounts of proceedings. Nonetheless, they were already interspersed with sporadic raids by the police during court sittings, records being seized and justices arrested. The Lord Mayor of Cork, Terence McSwiney, who was arrested while presiding at the District Court on 12 August 1920, died on hunger strike seventy-four days later.[16] In Wexford, when its mayor was arrested for a similar offence, aldermen, councillors and the law agent proceeded to the gaol and conducted municipal affairs there for several days, until their first citizen was released.[17]

Attitudes were hardening on both sides. There was pressure on office-holders to resign their honorary justiceships of the peace, and the IRA was imposing its own restricted licensing hours. However, the case of a Curracloe publican, charged at 'a Republican court' with selling drink to a certain farmer, having been forbidden to do so by the Irish Republican Police and of speaking contemptuously of the IRA, is a chilling aberration:[18] there was a conscious determination to keep the courts free of IRA domination. Even so, the courts were undoubtedly operating in a free-fall mode during these months. Not only did they have no rules, there was no judicial interpretation nor the check of an appellant forum. As Cahir Davitt wrote nearly fifty years later, 'There was as yet no prescribed code of law for them to administer, and there were no rules of court. Like the arbitration courts which had preceded them, they had for the most part to administer justice as they saw it and to regulate their own procedures.'[19]

The appointments of Crowley and Davitt took effect from 1 August 1920 and the first months were occupied in settling the Rules and Constitution of the courts at a series of meetings of all four judges: they also began to take Circuit sittings in Dublin, sometimes at the Technical Schools in Parnell Square or at the Court of Conscience in South William Street. Crowley and Davitt were anxious to get out into the country and to begin hearing cases there. The increasingly unsettled situation, with martial law in force over wide areas and the prosecution of all Sinn Féin activities, not only made the probable outcome of such a step dangerous, but likely to be ineffective because it could not be properly organised. Neither Meredith nor Clery saw it as a feasible development, but the other two were determined to try. Since Davitt had practised on the Western Circuit, it was thought proper that he should hear cases in the south and that Crowley would travel to the west and thus avoid any possible embarrassment in having cases in which they might have previously been instructed coming before them.[20]

The Ministry was unable to make any arrangements from Dublin, so Davitt set off for Limerick and called on the District Registrar, John McNeice, who worked as a solicitor's managing clerk there. They arranged dates for sittings in the city and county before Davitt journeyed on to Clare and Cork. He had considerable difficulty in establishing contact with the person in Cork whose name Stack had given him, because of the wariness generated by the fear of betrayal, and his lack of involvement with political or military figures left him no alternative contacts. In desperation, he called on Alfred O'Rahilly at University College Cork, whom he did not personally know but knew of him vaguely as being associated with the movement for independence. All Davitt had by way of identification was his father's watch, engraved 'Presented to Michael Davitt by the Irish Nationalists of Burnley District'. It was sufficient for O'Rahilly to promise that he would try and have someone get a message to Davitt at his hotel. He was eventually able to arrange the dates for Cork, but when he returned to Limerick he found that Cruise's Hotel, where he had retained a room on the outward journey, had been occupied by the military during his absence. He was almost betrayed by a drunken porter before he could extricate his luggage and effect a departure. In Limerick city he saw two District Judges, Stephen O'Mara, the Mayor, and Michael O'Callaghan, who was murdered a few months later. To get to the court in east Limerick entailed being passed along a line of guides and eventually to an IRA flying column, which delivered him to the house where the court was to be held. The Registrar turned out to be an acquaintance of Davitt's college days.

Cahir Davitt was the kingpin of the fledgling judicial system throughout Munster during the worst time of the Troubles and gave it an authority and status that could not have been achieved without some hierarchical framework which offered regulation and structure to the efforts being made on the ground. Davitt, travelling in secrecy and danger, and despite the incongruity of the makeshift courtrooms, brought in his person the *magisterium* of the law and showed the high seriousness with which local disputes and difficulties were regarded. That it may not have been thought through by the Ministry of Home Affairs is of secondary importance; it remains the reality of what Davitt did. Perhaps it was because he was so young that he was brave and serious, and the legal principles that he had been taught were still pristine; he carried out the task he was given with commendable grace and common sense. His youth undoubtedly helped in the often farcical contrast between his high office and the background against which it was exercised – such as travelling on a donkey and cart as the prospective son-in-law of the driver, sleeping between the District Registrar and the Brigade Officer, or finding himself in the middle of an ambush one evening. His position was respected by those into whose hands he was committed, even if he was once asked to leave a public house by the Republican Police because it was after the permitted hours.[21] While Davitt's attitude to his task was intellectual, pragmatic and detached, it was the impetuosity of Crowley, the older man, which was to prove a liability. There was no question of his physical courage, but he was emotional and headstrong. It was not only that he refused to take precautions, he invited confrontation with the Crown forces.

If Davitt's experience on this first outing as a Circuit Judge of the Dáil Courts is reminiscent of the French underground in World War II, Crowley's story is easily told. He had gone to Longford and thence to Ballina, where he insisted on sitting publicly; he then defied the police when they called on the court to disperse. Everyone was arrested: Crowley was subsequently sentenced to two years' hard labour by a military court and stripped of his British pension. He was not released until shortly before the Treaty[22] so that his grand gesture meant that Davitt was left to take whatever circuit sittings were possible to arrange during the darkest months of 'The Terror', as the period roughly between October 1920 and April 1921 came to be called by the nationalists. Davitt was satisfied that the secrecy in which the sittings were arranged and held was essential to safety. Even when the communication between the Ministry and a District Registrar was possible, the letters that survive show the precautions that were taken so as to leave the arrangements flexible and hidden. The Registrar was told that the Circuit Judge would be coming to his area on a certain date and the local man was to make the contact and arrange for the sittings.[23] Crowley's rashness in taking on the forces of the Crown and the futility of that defiance fade into theatricality, in contrast to Davitt's recollection that the only interference with his court were two occasions after the Truce by the RIC and once by an IRA officer after the Treaty: in answer to all three challenges, he had replied, 'This is a Court of the Irish Republic', and only the first time did he judge it wiser to have the court disperse.[24]

Not all courts had the good luck to avoid the more serious consequences of the attentions of the authorities. In January 1922, the Ministry refused to allow a payment of £1.14s. which had been made to a courts messenger in 1920 by the Parish Court of Currans and Currow, Co. Kerry, unless it got a full account of the revenue received over the same period. The three justices wrote back to attempt to give some idea of the difficulties under which they had tried to carry on, with scouts posted at strategic points to give warning if the military was in sight. The letter went on:

> To give an illustration of the severity of the military regime at the time, a court was to be held on the 14th December 1920. At the time appointed for the sitting of the court a party of four or five police and military officers drove up in a motor car and pulled up in front of the house wherein the court was to be held. Soon afterwards a large posse of police and military arrived in lorries from different points and surrounded the place of the intended sitting. Happily the Justices and litigants had not assembled at the time but had the Crown forces delayed half-an-hour longer, they would have caught the whole court sitting and what the consequences may be no one could tell. The house wherein the court was to be held was burned to the ground and four or five persons found in the vicinity of the place placed under arrest. Those persons were released after a few hours, with the exception of a man named John O'Connor, a litigant having a case, [who] was taken away on a lorry by the Crown forces and when some distance away was thrown from the tender and badly wounded. The unfortunate man was taken to a farmhouse nearby but the British forces again came back and dispatched him with revolvers. A haybarn in the locality was also burned on the same occasion ....[25]

It is impossible to get a coherent picture of the way the courts functioned in the period roughly between October 1920 and June 1921, partly because of the understandable absence of records and partly because many were unable to hold any sittings. From December 1920 all Munster was periodically under martial law, and while it is clear from the tragic story above that people did succeed from time to time to get a hearing for disputes, it is unlikely that the Republican Police were interested in prosecuting offenders. The files in the Public Records Office are the Ministry's, which means that we have the correspondence it received and the copies of letters it sent; its files were seized in a raid around December 1920, so even if there was any written communication (which is unlikely) it would have been lost. Moreover, Stack told Davitt in October 1920 that he would have to make his own contact direct with individual registrars, and Davitt himself, as we have seen, carried no written identification or authorisation. Some Parish Court books were sent to the Ministry in July 1922, but even they hardly would have been kept up to date.[26]

There is other evidence that the courts sat whenever and however they could during the worst of the Tan times, and that is principally in later references to decisions given in cases in 1920 and early in 1921. Father Punch of east Limerick said that only a day's notice of a court sitting was given for safety reasons. 'I was both registrar, judge and carrier of many summonses during the B. & T. campaign. Many people wanted the case adjourned in the hope that because of the Terror it might never be heard.'[27] The best documented case in the jurisprudence of the Dáil Courts – *Collins and Collins*[28] – developed from a judgement of the District Court in east Limerick given on 14 December 1920, four days after the county had been placed under martial law. Bridget Kennedy, the Registrar for west Limerick, furnished details of thirty cases which were dealt with between February and June 1921 and in which all the decrees, bar one, had been carried out.[29] Given the prosaic nature of the claims – recovery of debts, maintenance, rights of way – and the fact that even in ideal conditions the District Court was a monthly sitting, it was a surprising achievement. By March 1921, Cahir Davitt was on circuit again, first to Longford, then Clare, Limerick and Cork, and his recollection is of hearing a considerable number of cases, which presupposes that many of them were appeals. The same anonymity about his status and the location and time of the sittings was preserved, for this was well before the Truce:

> The Courts were held in all sorts of places. In the towns there were usually available halls of some kind or another, public buildings or schools, or Sinn Féin club premises. In the country districts recourse was had to creameries, farmhouses, outhouses, barns and any place with four walls and a roof that could be made ready and reasonably usable for the purpose.[30]

In fact, communication between the Minister and the registrars reopened a considerable time before the Truce, which began on 10 July 1921, and the presence of the circuit judge was being clamoured for by several areas.[31] Michael Collins intervened to reproach Stack for the lack of courts in south Cork and spoke of his own initiative in establishing contacts for the circuit judge. He was intent on harrying Stack and it is difficult to avoid the image of the local popular deputy pressurising the Minister, having taken only superficial soundings in his fiefdom. 'I take it you have no objection to the suggestion made that they should have a court. ... It seems to me that your Department should be the driving force in the move. ... I don't know if you are aware that litigants are being forced into British Courts entirely against their will through receiving no hearing from the people. ...'[32] It was a boorish and a bad blunder on the part of Collins. Cahir Davitt had sat in south Cork several weeks earlier and had already sent in his judgements dated 2 June and a letter about the case.[33] He would write notes in the evidence on loose papers or into small notebooks and post these to his mother in Dublin. Sometimes he would write out his Orders after the sittings if it were possible, or have the drafts typed in the Home Affairs office and sent down to the particular Registrar. Interestingly, he did not receive any complaint about the non-execution of the orders during the pre-Truce period.[34] For almost two months before Collins took issue with Stack about the courts in Cork, Davitt had been sitting in several districts in the county. The Registrar for north Cork, when furnishing his report of long sittings of the District Court in the first week of July, also pointed out that during the martial law period, only one or two cases usually could be heard at a time and it was impossible to keep records and difficult to collect fees.[35]

It can safely be assumed that the Dáil Courts had begun with something of a swagger in July 1920 as a graft on the structures in place for formal arbitration, that they sat openly until forced underground by increasing raids and arrests, and that they continued to be held when it was possible, or even more practically, when there was a need. Administration of civil justice by the statutory courts was also largely in suspension, but it is clear that the District Courts sat more frequently than is generally thought: such can be deduced, albeit somewhat patchily, from the files. We know considerably less about Parish Courts in the first months of 1921 but that was in the nature of the lines of command or communication which had been established. The parish clerks reported to the District Registrars, and if, for reasons of security, letters were no longer being sent, information we would otherwise have, even if it were only that gleaned from the complaints about the shortcomings of the parish clerks and the justices, is missing. The accounts of events at the local courts, which had been a regular feature in the newspapers, constitute a real gap because these supplied a barometer of the importance attached to them in the public interest. It has to be accepted that little can be discovered about the development of local courts at the most violent period of the Troubles, apart from the meagre information which managed to get recorded in the court books that survive.

It is sometimes thought that the courts had less impact in Dublin, either because the 'British' courts were able to continue to sit without interruption or that, because of the concentration of the Crown forces and the proximity of Dublin Castle, it would have been impossible to organise Dáil Court sittings there. However, merely to look at the catalogue of the records, one finds that the Winding-up Commission dealt with more than 600 cases in Dublin city and county.[36] The file of correspondence with Home Affairs in the years 1921/22 confirms that the courts were well organised there. Cahir Davitt recalled that all four judges held regular Circuit Courts at various venues in the Technical Schools at Bolton Street, Kevin Street and Parnell Square, as well as at the Court of Conscience, in September and October 1920.[37]

It was sometime after Christmas that the first sitting of the Supreme Court to exercise its original jurisdiction, rather than to hear appeals, was held.[38] Crowley being in prison, Davitt sat as the junior judge with Meredith and Clery. Apparently, Stack had intended that Arthur Clery was to be the President of the Supreme Court, but he had not given any direction to that effect. When the three filed onto the Bench, Davitt immediately made for the chair on the left as the most lowly. Counsel, solicitors and the public were on their feet. The other two judges stood there indecisive as to the order of precedence, and Davitt whispered to his friend and former professor, 'Go on, Arthur, take the Chair: you are the President,' but Clery was an extremely shy man and he simply went on vaguely nodding and smiling until Meredith broke the awkward impasse by taking the chair, on the grounds that he was the senior member of the Bar. It added to the piquancy of its image that James Creed Meredith became President of the Supreme Court of the Irish Republic because he was one of His Majesty's Counsels.[39] Meredith had been called to the Bar several years before Clery and it was perhaps fortunate that the nice observance barristers accord to such matters won through on this occasion, because Meredith had a natural authority and organising ability. By all accounts Arthur Clery was the beloved caricature of a professor – diffident, otherworldly, and slightly eccentric.[40] Although he was a respected legal scholar and a staunch Republican, he would hardly have made an effective President.

The courts in Dublin suffered no less from the attentions of the police and military, which led the parties in one case to find an exceptionally impudent venue for a court in which several of the witnesses were IRA officers wanted by the authorities. It was a claim for money for provisions supplied during the Easter Rising. Michael Noyk, one of the solicitors, booked a consultation room in the Solicitors Building in the Four Courts, and there the parties and witnesses assembled with Cahir Davitt, where the illegal court was held under the cover of a mundane legal consultation. It was the first time that the future President of the High Court was to sit in the Four Courts as a judge.[41]

Erskine Childers was a judge of the District Court for Pembroke and Rathmines and was concerned with the question of whether the court or the Minister of Home Affairs was in authority over the court personnel. Since he was the editor of the Dáil handbook on the subject – *The Constructive Work of Dáil Eireann – No. 1: The National Police and Courts of Justice* – it is surprising that he should be making enquiries as late as October 1921 about the arrangements, except that the letter has an air of pique, suggesting that there might have been a clash about some command.[42] He also asked whether they were unionised. The supreme irony is that they did not get around to a form of association until fifteen years later, when the courts had been closed for fourteen years, and the unfortunate Childers dead for as long.

The status of the courts in Dublin mirrored that over most of the country prior to the coming into operation of the Truce. They had begun with considerable stress on uniform organisation which presupposed they were going to be permitted to carry on without disruption. Within a short time, all those involved at a local level were driven to whatever makeshift arrangements were possible at any given time. By and large, records were not kept, for obvious reasons, or were destroyed deliberately by the enemy. There is enough evidence to show that they continued, however tenuously, to the extent of keeping the framework in place so that, even months before July 1921 and the cessation of hostilities, the separatist administration of justice began to emerge tentatively into the daylight once more with its self-confidence intact. It soared to the ridiculous extent of localised attempts to start up again in the Six Counties, which quixotic enterprise was actively urged on by Stack.[43] It was a brave effort, and some participants refused to accept that it was doomed until well into the following year. Elsewhere, as the ferocity of war diminished, litigants shook out their grievances and looked around for a forum in which to air them. They did not have far to look and every incentive was present to direct them into the Dáil Courts, the chief one being the absence of effective options. There were no juries for the Assizes, and local solicitors were now in more frequent attendance in the District and Parish Courts. A plaintiff had a better chance of having his claim heard, and. if successful, judgement executed there rather than in the County Courts. In addition, there was the growing tendency of defendants who were sued in a statutory court to apply before one of the professional judges for an injunction restraining the plaintiff proceeding against him in 'an enemy court'.[44] That it was used as a ploy to prevent a judgement justly deserved being effectuated, it goes without saying, but it must be noted, in view of the righteous outrage at the practice which came later, that such a patriotic stance was not only actively encouraged by Dáil Éireann, it was considered a betrayal to submit to the jurisdiction of a British Court.[45] In any case, to be shocked that a debtor might use any legal lacuna to avoid paying his debts is to demonstrate a *naïveté* unknown to practising lawyers the world over. Most people would take it for granted that a litigant might consciously seek the forum which he perceived – rightly or wrongly – as more likely to be favourable to his cause. The underlying strategy was not wholly prompted by mere self-interest: it was the stated policy of Sinn Féin that its own courts were to be used exclusively and it would have been seen as an act of patriotism to shun those operated by 'the enemy.'[46] In the end the practice came to be treated with some impatience by the professional judges, who alone had the power to grant the equitable relief of an injunction, and they insisted that an applicant must show that he had a *prima facie* defence to the claim being made against him and that the other side had prior notice of the application, before an injunction could be granted: and it was frequently refused.[47]

The underground courts were emerging here and there into the daylight several weeks before the Truce. Stack was already marshalling interest and anticipation for a more bureaucratic organisation of the courts. He castigated those justices who had not carried on regardless of suppression and arrest by the Crown forces, ignoring the lack of direction or initiative of his own department during the same period.[48] When he sent out details of the new scheme for organising the courts,[49] he urged that only those persons who would be prepared to serve whatever the danger were to be considered as potential justices. Elections were to take place in strict accordance with the rules. It was made clear that the role of the Sinn Féin clubs was that of support, loyalty and encouragement. Otherwise, only the Minister for Home Affairs and no other person had authority over the courts and court officials.[50] It was clear that the preliminary stage was considered at an end and that the Dáil Courts had evolved to having their administration directed from Dublin. Although there was nothing to indicate that Lloyd George was being prevailed upon by important personages to seek peace, unknowingly the ground was being prepared for the rapid consolidation of the courts which was to become strategically possible with the signing of the Truce.

4

The Truce:
An Honourable Understanding

When King George V opened the Northern Parliament, set up under the Government of Ireland Act 1920 on 22 June 1921, he used the occasion to urge 'a new era of peace, contentment and goodwill'. Three days later, Lloyd George wrote to de Valera inviting him to a conference with himself and Sir James Craig so that 'no endeavour should be lacking on our part to realise the King's prayer'. His initiative resulted in the Truce which came into effect on 11 July 1921. For most of the people it was a blessed relief from the sudden violent incident, military law and the curfew. The fighting men felt unease at the prospect of negotiations, and the political leaders warned against hopes being raised of a happy outcome. Austin Stack was among those who saw the Truce as a respite before the renewal of battle and also as an opportunity to advance substantially the legal system that he had set in motion. All concerned were to profit from the return to a more normal civilian life, and the British courts were not to be permitted to renew their former standing. It was imperative that the alternative being offered to the public would prove more efficient and accessible than the imperial legal administration which was, after all, open also to the benefits of the unexpected peace. Everything had to be done to encourage as many people as possible to bring their grievances to the Dáil Courts, and to this end the Ministry of Home Affairs became a kind of legal majordomo, channelling possible litigation from home and abroad to the relevant District Registrar, supervising its progress and responding sensitively to complaints from any source.[1] It is small wonder that the correspondence files for the post-Truce period far outweigh those of the post-Treaty period, when the Dáil Courts were at their peak.

The issue of courts did not feature in the scant terms of the Truce, nor was there any suggestion that it was considered at the time. Months later, on 21 October 1921, a White Paper was presented to Parliament where it was stressed that the Truce was the product of 'an honourable understanding' which was not embodied in a formal signed agreement. The communiqué issued by General Headquarters and that in the *Irish Bulletin* were set out, and while the latter gives a somewhat elaborate interpretation of conditions, they are 'identical in spirit', as the White Paper pointed out.[2] Yet, as early as 12 August, a Parish Court in Clare was dispersed by armed police on the grounds that such courts were political meetings under another guise, and that this broke the Truce. While the reverend chairman protested to Stack that it was 'just the ordinary cases',[3] no one averred to the absence of any interdict on political meetings either. In its essentials – and it was composed of nothing else – the agreement was to cease hostilities and a promise by the Irish 'to discontinue and prevent any action likely to cause a disturbance of the peace which might necessitate military interference'. The holding of courts mirroring those being held in all the villages and towns of England could hardly be intended to provoke a military reaction. The only provocation to breach the peace was coming from the Royal Irish Constabulary, who seized an opportunity to exercise a little muscle here and there before what they had left succumbed to inevitable atrophy. The police had been through a very bad time and the courts constituted a direct challenge to their authority. It was to be expected that the odd district inspector would try from time to time to face down those who had stolen his clothes. This was to be the pattern throughout the five months of the Truce.

Moreover, newspaper reports of the RIC raids had the same air of a set piece as those that had occurred in the summer of 1920. The police officer entered, the inspector or head constable queried the nature of the proceedings, and, on being told it was a Republican court, ordered that it be dispersed. He in turn would be asked if force would be used and invariably answered in the affirmative. A period of seeming intransigence would follow and then the presiding judge would direct that those present would leave quietly and at the same time make some observation to the effect that it was obvious which side was provoking a breach of the peace. The court would depart to assemble at an alternative venue and time, the police would remain in possesion for a period and each side could feel that virtue had triumphed. At the peace talks in London the fact that the courts were being held openly was an irritant to the British side as seeming to anticipate concession to a republic, which had already been ruled out. Lloyd George was upset to read that a court in Dublin had been declared open in the name of the Irish Republic and told his colleagues on 13 October, 'I shall have to tell them [the Irish delegation] that we shall have to scatter these courts.'[4] When the subject was raised later in the day with Griffith and Collins, assurances were given that something would be done.[5] However, Austin Stack made a note of de Valera's instructions to him:

> There is only one key to settling this question – methods of courts etc. must be unostentatious. The British must not [underlined] use their spies etc. to follow up and discover our Courts. The undertaking of the Truce is that they must wink if we work quitely [sic], if they follow us up and use force we shall have to use force to stave them off.[6]

It was advice that the Minister did not appear wholly to agree with, for he wrote to President de Valera on 2 November urging that everything should be done to bring disputes before Republican courts and that every assistance should be given to registrars and justices. As will be seen, it was some time later that he directed the courts to keep a low profile.

In the meantime, the newly invigorated ranks of District Registrars were forging ahead with the scheduling of courts, putting in requests for urgent circuit sittings and instructing parish clerks in the matters of procedure and weekly reports. It was also the Truce that brought the release of many judges and officials who had been imprisoned and the thorny question of the position of those who had replaced them. The Ministry was adamant that the former prisoners must be reinstated and the person who had been co-opted as a justice could continue to serve only as a substitute justice.[7] Bickerings broke out about the reformed election of justices: the worthy notion of maintaining a balance between capital – represented by farmers – and labour did little to prevent either side from trying to get as much representation as possible. Records were delved into in order to establish the ineligibility of a candidate and, of course, the Ministry was appealed to by all parties.[8] Being a justice had an enviable status in the parish and consequently attracted the malice which assuages envy. In a society reeling from savagely imposed partisanship, the easiest of all suggestions was past collaboration with the enemy. The advent of peace and sovereignty did not secure immunity. As late as the spring of 1922 a well-liked justice in east Limerick was dismissed when papers found in a raid revealed that he was among those farmers who had petitioned the military commander in 1920 to extend the curfew for one hour so that the harvest might be brought in.[9]

Stack wrote to some registrars complimenting them on the fact that their courts had continued during the worst of the Terror: he told them that he had brought their work to the attention of the Dáil,[10] but he routinely objected to whatever sum the District Judges decided to pay them, while irritatingly repeating that it was a matter for the judges to decide, but for him to sanction.[11] It was almost as if there were a self-regulating Treasury built into the Ministry, since it protested every item of expenditure, in a manner that was to be reflected in the relationship of the Ministry of Finance and that of Home Affairs two years later about the estimates for the cost of the Dáil Courts Winding-up Commission: except, of course, that in the operation of the local courts, it was income which they themselves had generated, and not Dáil funds.

A brave attempt was made to get the courts revived in Northern Ireland, now a separate political entity, but it had little hope of success given the political realities of partition. The records for north Tyrone from July onwards show that justices had been appointed but 'the court never got the chance of impressing the people'. The Minister's informant also regretted the loss to the British courts of a 'large amount of cases of trespass, compensation claims, assault and threatening language, most of which occur amongst Republicans'.[12] Not only did the courts fail to capture this lucrative business before the Truce, but Eamon Donnelly, who was the organiser for all Northern Ireland, was unable to report any real progress.[13] There was a flurry of excitement in mid-Tyrone when a parish clerk was arrested – by the IRA. Home Affairs intervened through the Dáil Ministry of Defence to ask that he be allowed to return to his duties, but word came back that permission had been sought to have the man executed. 'In view of this you will note the impossibility of acceding to the request for his release.'[14] It was different for the solicitors in Derry City, who could use the District Court in Carndonagh across the border in Donegal.[15] The political realities of the Northern situation prevented the Dáil Courts from winning the kind of acceptance by the community which they had in the South.

By August 1921 reports of cases heard began to reappear in local newspapers, and moreover, the contrast between the busy Parish Courts and the Petty Sessions, made barren by lack of litigants and witnesses, was once again being highlighted. It was unlikely that this open display of a usurping legal system, when some men were still serving prison sentences for their association with it, would go unremarked. The litany of outraged questions was resumed in the House of Commons. Colonel Gretton, who had to endure the added insult of having his Bass beer boycotted under Sinn Féin principles,[16] wanted to know if the Sinn Féin Courts were expressly dealt with in the terms of the Truce. However, the usual placebo of the government reply – that arbitration courts to which the parties came willingly were not illegal – only further irritated Sir Frederick Banbury, who exploded: 'Are we to understand that arbitration courts, set up by the rebels have been sanctioned by the Government?' While it is difficult to imagine the military mind being much troubled by civilian courts disposing of civilian disputes or bringing the local miscreant to justice, the support of officers was canvassed by one side or another. The British Liaison Officer in Galway protested to Eamonn Duggan, the Chief Liaison Officer, that an ejectment decree against a woman had been executed but the Crown forces had gallantly intervened. Stack was furious: 'With as much, if not more, justice we might say that the English Sheriffs in this court are not entitled to execute Decrees of the British Courts. If the matter is referred to me for a direction I shall instruct our police to re-eject this woman who took fraudulent possession of the premises on the advice of the enemy.'[17] Obviously, the Truce did not ensure that a plain citizen would no longer be caught in the crossfire, even when it was, mercifully, confined to words.

Austin Stack, in his ministerial report of 16 August 1921, was able to write that the courts were operating again in every part of the country.[18] A week before he had circulated all registrars with details of the new scheme of organisation, specimen District Court forms, several copies of a memorandum on costs, expenses and deposits, as well as on jurisdiction. In addition, the Clerk of the Dáil was asked for assistance in sending on similar circulars to every deputy, as well as copies of *The*

Judiciary with a letter urging that if the scheme was put into operation, the success of the courts was ensured and that there was 'nothing the Enemy can do to break them.'[19] They were enlisted to keep an eye out for failure and neglect. Where elections had not been held under the rules or justices had been co-opted informally during the bad times, there was an insistence that fresh elections were to take place. It was also stressed that only men willing to carry on even if martial law were to be reimposed were to be considered eligible. There was more than a suggestion that had justices not proved so pusillanimous, many more courts would have carried on in the face of suppression. It was not merely illogical: it was also a mite disingenuous from a man who had claimed in his recent report that the courts had fallen into abeyance owing to enemy action and the arrests of justices and officials.[20] However, it may have been his clumsy way of 'rallying the troops': there seems to have been a good deal of the scoutmaster in Stack.

Moreover, in the midst of all this resurgence, he persisted in seeking court returns for the period ending July 1921. It was, of course, unreal: those who had escaped imprisonment, or even death, were unlikely to do so with complete sets of records. Indeed, they would have put themselves in further jeopardy if documents were discovered. Imprisonment for up to two years was imposed on persons found with papers that led a court martial to the conclusion that they had been involved in a subversive court.[21]

Even solicitors considered it unsafe to keep records, as a Sligo solicitor was to point out two years later to the Winding-up Commission: 'For obvious reasons, solicitors kept no records of cases tried in the Dáil Éireann Courts during a considerable period. It would have been dangerous for the solicitor and for the people for whom he acted as well as officials of the courts.'[22] The Ministry must have appreciated that the situation was in most places that described by Seamus Breathnach, Registrar for south-east Cork: 'With reference to court work from the inception of the Courts to July 31, the records for this particular period are of such fragmentary nature owing to the disturbed state of the country that it is impossible at present to write anything like an intelligible report. I may mention that one of my predecessors is in penal servitude, another is interned, and there is no account of the third.'[23] It did not stop the demands being made, perhaps being prompted by financial rather than statistical curiosity. One registrar mentioned that some parish clerks were arrested with court fees on them and that until their release the position could not be ascertained: the ink was barely dry on the signatures of the plenipotentiaries in London before the Ministry was pointing out that the whereabouts of the money could now be discovered.[24] The clerks were freed with the money intact, which must be to the credit of the Crown forces whom history credits with so little.

Austin Stack made the expansion of the courts during the Truce a point of honour. He may have even been disappointed that it was a principle that, happily, no one was prepared to risk imprisonment for. There occurred a series of minor incidents, mostly sparked off by some coat-trailing, so the only problem was that of saving face. While the Ministry did issue a General Instruction to registrars and clerks on the possibility of a confrontation, it did so as late as 24 November 1921,[25] and then, probably as a reaction to a determined campaign by Divisional Inspector Scully of the RIC in north Dublin to force the issue. Officials were instructed to conceal the time and venue of the courts as far as possible, but justices were to adjourn only if actual force was used to disperse it: former instructions were to be ignored if they were contrary to the present circular. Frank Harding, who was Registrar for north Dublin, had confirmed in early November that most of the parish court sittings took place in their local Carnegie Library[26] but the Ministry instructed by return of post that the Balbriggan court was not to be held in the public library. Two days before, Inspector Scully had lodged a complaint that a court would be held in the Carnegie Library at Balbriggan where a publican from Balrothery would be prosecuted for serving drink on a Sunday during hours prohibited by 'some order alleged to have emanated from your headquarters'.[27] Presumably he meant from the Irish Republican Police. 'As this is a distinct breach of the Truce, I request that you give this matter your careful and immediate attention', which, in view of the advance notice, turned out to be the simple expedient of changing the venue. There must be few other occasions in history where a truce between warring parties was considered violated by the curtailment of Sabbath drinking hours. The redoubtable inspector did succeed in dispersing a parish court at Rush instead of the following week.

What is surprising is the lateness of the hour when the incidents of disruption were still occurring. Cahir Davitt was taking a sitting of the court in the upper floor of shop premises at Maudabawn in east Cavan when a district inspector and several constables arrived to query the status of the court. Judge Davitt said it was not arbitration: it was a Court of the Republic. After a private conference with the lawyers present, it was agreed to adjourn rather than allow themselves to be dispersed by force, which had been threatened, albeit politely; the date was 22 November 1921.[28] Davitt returned to Dublin to seek instructions from Stack, who was of the opinion that the RIC had no governmental authority to disperse court sittings by force. It was agreed that, should a similar visitation take place, the judge would not adjourn but face down the police. The opportunity to test the strategy presented itself in a court in Monaghan about a week later, when a head constable again said that he would disperse the court if it was not done voluntarily. Davitt directed that the cross-examination which had been in progress should continue, a direction which counsel obeyed with understandable nervousness. The officer retreated to the end of the hall with his men and remained there for about a half-hour, but did not attempt any further interruption. Although Cahir Davitt had a very heavy workload from before the Truce until the Treaty, taking circuit sittings in at least eight counties as well as Dublin, these were the only attempts made to interfere with his court. He was demonstrably a man of cool courage, because, after the incident in Maudabawn, the District Registrar feared for Davitt's safety. He warned the Ministry that when the Judge returned to the area, his travel arrangements should be changed: 'If he comes to Cootehill, he will be shadowed and in all probably [*sic*] be run down.'[29] Davitt makes no mention of the threat in his recollections, although Stack passed on the letter to him a few days later.

The plans laid by Stack in early June 1921 and his instinct that the heavy arm of the law would be held in check rather than undertake a policy of suppressing the courts by violence – and their visible resurgence showed that previous policy had not been an unalloyed success – placed the Ministry for Home Affairs in the position of a quasi-populist network widespread throughout the country; it could impress a captive audience with the attributes of a centralised authority. It is not without significance that Erskine Childers, in his publicist series *The Constructive Work of Dáil Eireann,* led off with *The National Police and Courts of Justice (Ministry of Home Affairs).* Having given an outline of the arrest and imprisonment of those working in the courts, and of the raids and seizure of documents, he summarised the pre-Truce situation:

> The effect, as might be supposed, was to curtail the activities of the courts and to compel them to hold their sittings in secret, but not to destroy them or the fabric of the judicial system embodied in them. A considerable curtailment, especially of the work done by the police, was in any case inevitable owing to the steady intensification of the war of independence throughout the whole period, until the Truce of July 11th, 1921, was declared. War and civil justice co-exist with some difficulty at the best.[30]

The records bear out the truth of the first sentence, although Childers could not have known at the time that the Dáil judicial system was about to expand in several directions. It would shortly be apparent that the period of which he was speaking would prove to be a hiatus. Reports from the registrars confirmed the regular functioning of parish courts in the months of July and August and the demands for the services of Judge Davitt to hear circuit cases and appeals. Crowley was still in prison, but Meredith and Clery could now venture out in a safer climate to exercise their alternative jurisdiction as circuit judges in other locations than in Dublin.[31] Davitt, who alone had borne the heat of the day and travelled with stoic good humour into places of constant danger, was in a position to assess close up the difference in the operation of the courts from the summer of 1921. Because his whole narrative is characterised by a judicious restraint and although descriptive and wryly humorous, he religiously avoids subjectivity, his summary of the post-Truce courts is therefore all the more valuable and deserves to be quoted at some length:

> The period between the Truce and the Treaty was marked by an immense increase in the volume of the Circuit Sittings over which I presided. Litigants took advantage of the cessation of hostilities to resort in greater numbers to the Courts, and counsel and solicitors appeared more frequently. There was uninterrupted communication between the District Court Registrars in the country and Ministry for Home Affairs; and the arrangement of Circuit Sittings presented no difficulty. The result was a great expansion of business at Circuit

Sittings. During this period I appear, from the records I have, to have disposed of some hundred and thirty-five cases. These included appeals from the District Courts at ordinary sittings as well as cases heard at first instance. They were of all kinds and descriptions, almost every type of claim in equity or at common law being represented. There were will suits and suits for the administration of estates, suits for declarations as to the ownership of land and other property, suits for specific performance and to set aside and rectify deeds, actions for breach of promise of marriage and for judicial separation, actions for assault, slander, trespass, trover and conversion, detinue, breach of contract, breach of warranty, work and labour done, money had and received, money due on promissory note, ejectment, rent, and so forth and so on. Apart from the appeals, most of them were very substantial cases. In several the amount involved exceeded the thousand pounds and in most many hundreds were at stake.[32]

Father David Fitzgerald, the chairman of the Abbeyfeale Parish Court, sent a cutting from the *Cork Examiner* dated 30 November 1921 reporting that his court had been interrupted by a district inspector, a head constable, two sergeants and five constables. By sheer coincidence, the court happened to be dealing with an arbitration matter, but the inspector had said that they had instructions to disperse all other courts. There can be no doubting the writer's bewilderment: 'Your Department can hardly sanction the probable violation of the Truce in every Parish Court in Ireland. ... We would not violate the Truce one iota if we considered we were committing a breach of it.'[33] Stack had little patience with this truce abiding cleric. 'A Chara urranaigh,' he replied, 'We are the Government of the country and as such are entitled to try all kinds of cases in our Courts.'[34] The sad irony was that the following day, that is, 6 December, it was finally agreed that the country would have its own government – and courts – but Austin Stack was never to be a part of it.

5

The Light of Day

The outcome of the Treaty talks was greeted with widespread relief throughout the country. Newspaper headlines and leading articles testify to this. The peace that people had become accustomed to was not going to be shattered further. The British would leave, and the Irish would have their own government and could get on with their lives. As F.S.L. Lyons has put it, in words that describe the reaction of civilians everywhere when hostilities end: 'Ordinary people, who wanted only to be allowed sleep quiet of nights and earn an honest living, probably saw no further than that this had suddenly become possible; for them, and for many others, the immediate release of prisoners held by the British authorities was a fact more potent than any abstract conception of an ideal, but unrealisable republic.'[1] Or as one of the participants in those talks, Winston Churchill, wrote: 'No one was more delighted than the poor, ordinary people of Ireland who had been so mauled by both sides and who longed for peace and comfort.'[2] In so far as the same ordinary people thought about courts at all, they had every reason to assume that, with native government, the courts set up and nurtured by the men now coming into their own, and which had all but eclipsed the official courts at every level, were set not only to continue, but to enter upon their kingdom. The antagonism towards the former administration of justice was pervasive, bound up as it was with colonial perceptions on both sides. It explains the comment about the judges who had formerly acted under British authority in Ireland in a letter written by Hugh Kennedy to the Minister for Home Affairs on 17 January 1922: 'Orders suppressing national, political and even literary organisations will be found over the signatures of the members of this Judiciary. So they have departed from the status of independence of executive government by taking a hand in its work ... poison in the well of justice in this country.'[3] He thought the Provisional Government should consider warning the judges not to interfere in public business and hoped that the recently issued Proclamation sufficiently covered this point.

Kennedy was not only the government's legal adviser; he was a King's Counsel, and the proclamation to which he referred had been issued the previous day. It announced that the Provisional Government had entered upon the functions of its office and directed that the law courts and all public bodies, which had acted under the authority of the British government, were to continue in operation until the establishment of the Free State.[4] This announcement, which appeared in the public press on 17 January 1922, was to cause confusion, anger and resentment, but the debate in the Dáil which preceded it had ended with the bitter division into pro- and anti-Treatyites and eventually led to the abolition of the Dáil court system.

The Dáil had assembled on 14 December 1921 to consider the Anglo-Irish agreement, and after one secret session and twelve sittings, the vote was taken on 7 January: sixty-four deputies were in favour and fifty-four against. De Valera resigned as President of the Republic and so did Austin Stack as Minister for Home Affairs. When Arthur Griffith was elected President on the vote that followed, he vowed to keep the Republic in existence until an election was held and the Free State established.[5] He formed a new ministry in which Eamonn Duggan took over Home Affairs. While the Dáil and its ministries continued a parallel existence, a special meeting for 14 January was called for the parliament of Southern Ireland – that is, the parliament provided for under the Government of Ireland Act 1920, and which, apart from the four Dublin University members, had heretofore sat as the Dáil.[6] The purpose of the present meeting was to elect a provisional government in accordance with Articles 17 and 18 of the Treaty. Collins, as chairman, was head of the Provisional Government, and Duggan held the same ministry under him as he did in the Dáil: so did the other members of the government, except for Eoin McNeill and Finian Lynch. However, the responsibilities attached to Duggan's office are of particular interest. They included only those functions of judicial administration associated with Dublin Castle – such as the Lord Chancellor's secretariat, Probate, Land and Deeds Registries and the police: the Dáil court system naturally was not a function that could be transferred by the British. *The raison d'être* of the Provisional Government was to take over the functions of administration until a general election could be held. Duggan was the only member to have an assistant Minister: George Nicholls was appointed on 17 January, officially to take charge in Mr Duggan's absence,[7] but his only function was to direct the Dáil Ministry of Home Affairs at 22 Dawson Street, which was kept distinct from the government Ministry at Upper Merrion Street (later to become the Department of Justice). It was a matter of policy to preserve the official *cordon sanitaire* that separated the government from the courts that operated in every parish within its jurisdiction. The fiction provided a discreet crutch for Winston Churchill, who was forced to answer awkward questions in the Commons on this ostensible breach of the Treaty in the months ahead, as would soon transpire.

Nicholls had already written to the District Registrars on 13 January with his instructions to make arrangements for the Circuit Court sitting in their areas,[8] but three days later, they read that the established courts were to continue to operate, as if the past two years had not happened. There was a flood of letters in response. Liam Sweeney of south Donegal wrote a long and explosive denunciation:

> I was sure that every justice, judge and clerk would work on under the Provisional Government when the bombshell came, and of all the unexpected sources, from the Government itself. I refer to the first Order of the new Government which appeared in the papers on Tuesday morning, e.g. 'that all public bodies including the Law Courts (British) should continue to function etc.' ... parish justices were as honest in dealing with petty cases as the men who had J.P. behind their names and an oath of allegiance to England on their conscience. ...
>
> Those who had put themselves in danger and had worked for nothing to do the work of law and order were going to be passed over in favour of those who never did a stroke of work for Ireland in their lives. ... I want to be able to tell Registrars, Judges, Justices and others that our Courts are going to go on, that the rights of individuals will be seen to, that it is the party who made the Free State a possibility that is still the advising party: or that the new Government does not want our

aid any more, and that, having done the work in danger and hardship, in times of peace and prosperity, we go. Which am I to tell them?[9]

The officer in charge of the Republican police in Monaghan enquired of his chief, 'Am I to allow people to enter British courts which have been debarred to them previous to the Treaty, or am I to allow the British Summons and Civil Bill officers to function in the same way as they did previous to the establishment of the Republican Courts?'[10] When J.G. Hassett, one of the justices for the district of Mid-Tipperary, expressed his bewilderment in the face of the conflicting orders, the Assistant Minister replied: 'As the Republic and the Republican Government still stands, orders and instructions issued by the Provisional Government have no influence in any way on Republican Court officials. The Republican Courts shall continue to function as heretofore and all necessary steps must be taken to boycott the Enemy Courts until the Irish people approve of the Free State Government. Our position remains unchanged and the Republican Courts are the only legal courts of the Irish people.'[11]

Those who had collectively made the subversive courts of the Republic a reality in every town outside the north-east corner of the country, had reason to be apprehensive when the priority of the successful revolutionaries appeared to be the regeneration of the courts they had brushed aside. If that were so, where was their place to be in the new order? The Proclamation had gone on to forbid the dismissal of any official, so that would have closed the prospect of employment in corresponding positions in the court service to those registrars and clerks. A great number of lay justices stood to lose their status in the local community. The volte-face with which they all had seemingly been presented set at nought the risk of imprisonment, loss of livelihood and even death which they had faced during the previous two years, not to speak of the constant harassment from their own leaders on the importance of preserving the public from the contamination of the 'enemy courts'. The reassurance they were now receiving from the same quarter would have had a decidedly hollow ring, except to ears anxious to hear the orthodoxy of native innovation confirmed. After all, George Nicholls, who was giving the seditious instructions that no notice be taken of the specific commands of the Provisional Government, and that the Republican courts were the only legal ones, was at the time asking instructions of the same government about whether or not he should proceed with the preparations for the holding of the Assize Courts.[12]

It was as if all concerned kept their minds rigidly compartmentalised on the issue of structures for the administration of justice within the State. The Proclamation had merely outlined what had been agreed in the Treaty, the contents of which were being argued on a line-by-line basis at that time in discussions in London. When Kevin O'Higgins and Eamonn Duggan were crossing over to London on 17 January for this purpose, they were instructed to enquire about 'the British view regarding the Judiciary'.[13] Patrick McGilligan went with them as secretary, and there is a pencilled note which suggests that O'Higgins asked if prosecutions would have to be taken in the name of the King during the provisional period, and that Hamar Greenwood confirmed that it was so.[14] There was clearly a difficulty in drafting the commission under which the Assize Judges would go out – perhaps because the role of the monarch as the source of judicial authority, and not the people, would thus be ungainsayable – and the matter was raised at cabinet on six near-consecutive days.[15] The Under-Secretary, James McMahon, at the Castle and Judge Wylie were both consulted, but the problem must have proved insoluble, because it ended in a terse instruction that Duggan was to see that the Assizes did not go out. If they had gone out, it might have answered the question from where their 'clientele' was to come. Only a week before, on 20 January, it had been decided by the Provisional Government that the Republican courts were to continue and that persons sentenced there were to be housed in government prisons.[16] This should have made the criminal jurisdiction of the older courts redundant, if it were not already. Who was to compile the lists for the grand juries and what might the attitude of the IRA be to the reappearance of the King's judges? From whose ranks would the dignitaries and police be recruited to furnish the customary entourage? Perhaps it was concluded that the difficulties were too great; in any event, the question of courts, royal or revolutionary, was not raised again at the cabinet level until 8 March, and even then consideration of the concurrent jurisdiction of the courts was deferred.[17]

Why was it deemed so vital to preserve not merely the myth, but the quasi-reality of the Republic, of which the outward and visible signs of the Army and the Courts loomed so large? The lengthy Dáil debate had made it clear that a republic was not on offer, hence the split, but no attempt was made to use any other word to describe the courts except 'Republican', though they were to be referred to in subsequent legislation, and correctly, as the Dáil Courts. Equally, the Army was the Irish Republican Army, at least up to the crisis of the Army Convention in March. It speaks volumes for the sober and steady progress of the courts that there was no parallel disruption: it may explain why the government, preoccupied with the coming elections, events in the North and the looming threats of both de Valera's opposition and the Irish Republican Army, ignored them for so long. Moreover, it had not been expected that the formal establishment of the Free State would take as long as a year, because the election provided for in the Treaty was intended to take place much earlier than it did. Three drafts of the proposed Constitution, incorporating a new court system, were submitted to the Provisional Government on 7 March 1922.[18] Deliberations and discussions in Dublin and negotiations on its terms in London succeeded in delaying its publication until the same day as the much-procrastinated general election – 16 June 1922. Had there been no dissension on the Anglo-Irish Treaty and events had moved smoothly in harmony with its terms, it was theoretically possible for the courts of the Free State to open the new law term in October 1922. It may explain why no steps were taken to confront the question of two jurisdictional imperatives. After all, the government did not establish a committee to advise on the new judical system until the following September. Neither does it explain the failure to recognise the legal rights and duties of litigants springing from the judgements of Dáil Courts into which they had been led and herded by those now in power. In any event, nothing happened according to the optimistic timescale; furthermore, the courts of the Free State did not come into existence until eighteen months after its establishment. And before that, the government was to pay for its folly by being forced to reactivate the Dáil courts by means of a judicial commission, as we shall see, so that decisions at even parish court level became *res judicata* (a matter already decided) under the particular jurisdiction of the High Court of Saorstat Éireann.

Davitt was acutely conscious of the anomalous position of the courts in which he was serving with such distinction, and he saw the way it could have been avoided:

In implementing the Treaty, the Dáil should have unequivocally provided for the transfer to the Provisional Government of all the functions of the government of the Republic; the Dáil of 1922 had as much authority from the people to do this as had the Dáil of 1919 to set up the Republic in the first instance; amongst the functions of the British Government here which were transferred to the Provisional Government was the administration of justice, and the whole machinery of the 'British Courts', as they were termed, was taken over and became part and parcel of the government machinery under our own control; the decision to carry on both governments at the same time saddled the country with two systems of judicature which were mutually incompatible.[19]

It is difficult to fault the eminent good sense of what Davitt suggests would have been the better course, but it is a pity that he gives no hint of why a decision which he considered to be 'a grave political error' was taken. Neither does he seem to have considered that in voting for the Treaty, the Dáil had effectively voted itself out of existence. When it ratified the appointment of the Ministers of the Provisional Government, it signalled the suspension of parliamentary democracy until another election was held. The British government was adamantine in its insistence that it alone empowered the ministers to govern during the transitional period. Both Griffith and Collins had equally insisted that Provisional Government ministers were not responsible to the Dáil: it is not without irony that they did so during a debate there on 28 February,[20] which begs the question of why it was being maintained. Perhaps in the hope that civil war might be waged by other means. Whatever the purpose of the maintenance of the Dáil, it had no power to make government answerable to it. Within the week of the Treaty being signed, Kennedy had noted that the 'Provisional Government is for purposes of administration only', and in the same series of brief memoranda, 'the purpose for which it is being set up, viz. administration, will control its operations and that it will not function in the full sense as a Parliament'.[21] One wonders why he added the qualification – it could not function as a parliament at all.

Whatever the jurisdictional doubts, the courts established by the decree of the First Dáil in 1920 now entered into an era of uninterrupted expansion. The impediment of the 16 January proclamation was thereafter ignored and the Circuit List prepared for the spring sittings in the towns of Munster, Leinster and Connacht. Extra judges such as Lavery, Flood, Wyse Power and Goff were given temporary commissions in order to deal with the pressure of cases waiting to be heard. Creed Meredith and Arthur Clery, of the Supreme Court, also went out on circuit and all judges were accompanied by registrars chosen by themselves.[22] Within one month, Davitt alone had disposed of more than a hundred cases, but as early as 28 January the *Kerry People* had reported that the District Court in Tralee had sat an entire day to hear civil cases.[23] It was noted in the *Clare Champion* on 11 February that the Parish Court had sat in the Ennis courthouse on the basis that 'they had a right to hold it in a proper courthouse'.[24] There were occasional reports of incidents in which IRA officers appeared at sittings of Petty Sessions or a County Court to issue a challenge to their jurisdiction, but no force appears to have been used. Davitt recalled that in Kerry he was asked by one such officer whether his court was a Republican or Free State one. When he gave the same answer he had given before the Treaty – that it was a court of the Irish Republic – the man withdrew.[25]

Aside from the implied threat, the question would seem to have been pertinent, but reading newspaper accounts, the only persons who seemed prepared to raise it publicly were either in the IRA or in the British House of Commons. It was a fairly regular source of query in that place; for example, Captain Foxcroft MP asked if Republican courts were sitting openly, presided over in one case by a King's Counsel. Churchill confirmed that this was so in areas not fully under the control of the Provisional Government, adding that he saw 'the impropriety of allowing illegal courts to fine or imprison His Majesty's subjects',[26] ignoring the obvious conclusion that, somehow, prisons were being provided and fines collected. If he made private representations to the Irish government on the subject at any time, they are not among the record of the many representations that he did make during this period.

In his report of 27 February 1922, George Nicholls gave an enthusiastic account of the success of the courts now that past difficulties which 'had retarded the working of the courts have altogether disappeared … the Department has been in a position to arrange Spring sittings of the Circuit Courts which can only be described as phenomenal'.[27] Already, though, considerable strain was developing amongst those working in

the department because of factional differences over the Treaty. Dan
Browne, Madge Clifford, Kathleen Bulfin and Eamon Burke formed the
permanent staff of the Dáil Court Section: they had been personally
recruited by Austin Stack and like him were all from Kerry. In his report
in January to the official Home Affairs Ministry, Nicholls, with a rare
display of humour, described the department which he had inherited as
'truly a department of Home Affairs'.[28] He felt that the staff were watching
him closely to see if he planned to betray the Republic and reporting back
to Stack. He decided to bring in a second fifth column to undermine the
first. J.M. Maxwell was prevailed upon through an intermediary to release
two law clerks in the employment of his firm, Maxwell Weldon and
Company, Solicitors, to work in Nicholls' office. The two were Padraic
Crump and Owen McKeon, and while it was inconvenient, Maxwell
patriotically agreed 'to recognise that private matters must give way to
the necessities of State'.[29] He must have been persuaded that the State was
being served by increasing the numbers of persons administering non-
statutory courts. Even judged from the viewpoint of the courts themselves,
they were well served by the existing staff, of whose devotion to the work
there had never been any doubt, whatever about their loyalty to the new
order. It can be assumed that *their* position would have been that the
courts did not belong to the new order. Surprisingly, Crump was later to
complain that, apart from Browne, the rest of the staff ignored him.[30] He
moved rapidly up the ladder of seniority, however, because most of the
pre-Treaty staff left to rally around de Valera; first, Madge Clifford and
Burke, and then, on 22 March, Browne resigned.

Dan Browne was the solicitor who had been Secretary of the Dáil
Ministry since Stack's time. He was an experienced and respected
administrator whose communications were always addressed directly to
Duggan as Minister. In his letter of resignation, he told Duggan, 'I cannot
agree that it is the policy of the present Government to preserve those
Courts: rather do I think they appear anxious for their overthrow'.[31] He
had decided to support de Valera in the coming elections and that was the
immediate cause of his leaving. The wording is open to the construction
that the matter of the courts had already been discussed between the
two men. It had been raised in the Dáil cabinet – of which the Minister
was a member – on 24 February, when the Assistant Minister had
sent a communication, and later Mr Browne had written a letter: once

more a decision was deferred.[32] As usual, we do not know what form the discussion took, who spoke, or what the letter said. It has already been noted that the same procedure was re-enacted at the government meeting of 8 March, when Mr Duggan was to circulate a memorandum:[33] no development is recorded, nor is there such a memorandum in the cabinet papers. However, there is an undated and unsigned copy of a memorandum in Hugh Kennedy's papers, which he might have prepared for Duggan to present to the government around this time.[34]

It begins by advising the government not to take any action that would have the effect of extending the jurisdiction of the Republican courts, nor should their existence be maintained. The writer recommends that the High Court and County Court should take over the work done by the Supreme Court and District Court respectively, and reformed Petty Sessions, presided over by 'Sinn Féin men with legal training', should replace the Parish Courts. It continues, 'the Ministry has fortunately the power to terminate their existence legally by rescinding the Order constituting them: it should exercise that power at once'. Here is the Law Adviser giving legitimacy to the recognition of the continuing Republic by pointing the way the courts could be 'legally' closed down within the parameters of their Dáil Éireann origins. As Davitt pointed out, the administration of justice was in the hands of the government: why not decree that, on a given date, all matters before the Dáil Courts would be transferred into the jurisdiction of the statutory courts? In fact, Meredith was to present a draft decree along the same lines which will be referred to later. In practice, it should not have worked any great injustice: the law, pleadings and legal practitioners would have been the same: only the identities of the judges would have changed. Perhaps that was the real sticking point, that the politicians knew that the public would no longer accept that their grievances would be disposed of by Crown-appointed judges. But had this course been chosen, there would have been considerably less injustice suffered by litigants at the end of the day than the chaos into which they were plunged by the unwise and hasty action taken later on.

Duggan's reply to Browne was one of the rare occasions when the convention that these courts had nothing to do with him was dropped. It was a measure of Browne's standing that the Minister crossed out part of the official draft and wrote in his own hand:

It is within your knowledge that it is altogether due to the policy of the present Government that the activity of the Courts has so immeasurably increased of late, with a consequent increase in the measure of departmental work. I must observe that you do not appear to have considered the serious effect on the efficiency of the Courts, which a sudden dislocation of the office entails. I should at least have thought that an official with your views would have a better appreciation of the vital interest and welfare of the Courts.[35]

T. V. Cleary was the only one of the original staff, apart from organizers, to remain in the Ministry of Home Affairs after April 1922, but since he was Supreme Court Registrar and worked from the offices at 13 Wellington Quay, he had not much contact with other staff and corresponded direct with the judges and their registrars. He certaintly exhibited no great cordiality towards Nicholls and Crump, but they were to have their revenge, as we shall see in the next chapter. Whatever the antagonisms at headquarters or the doubts at the cabinet table, the operation of the courts was unaffected by them. Indeed, there were indications that seemed to confirm their permanancy.

The Chief Secretary's Office at Dublin Castle continued to function to the extent of dealing with matters arising during the transitional period.[36] The Registrar of Petty Session clerks, whose office was also at the Castle, was inundated with complaints from clerks for Petty Sessions that Parish Courts had taken over the court houses without force or threat often by the simple expedient of being there first.[37] They told stories of being kindly handed their books and records, or being told that they could hold their Petty Sessions when the business of the usurping court was finished. The Resident Magistrates had the same tale to relate to the Under-Secretary, James McMahon.[38] They were all instructed to make representations 'to the local representative of the Provisional Government with a view of having the matters complained of remedied as far as possible', but if the identity or whereabouts of any such official was known (even had he existed) to Dublin Castle, they were not told. The Ministry of Home Affairs was formally apprised of the situation – it could scarcely have been startling news – but there was no change and it was tacitly accepted that there would not be. In any case, the days of the Resident Magistrates were numbered and it must have borne in on them gradually, since no one took the trouble to tell them.[39] Their letters hold 'future echoes' – if such a concept were possible – of the ending of the British Raj, and it is difficult not to feel that they were shabbily treated by the representatives of the former masters whose interests they had loyally served. Major Herries-Crosbie had intended to retire: 'I can hardly ask for work in purely Republican Courts – or accept it if offered'.[40] J.B. Hill, RM, was isolated in County Galway where the RIC was pulling out of the barracks on a daily basis. The magistrate at Collon, County Louth had no illusions:

> Republican Courts function everywhere and do all the work, civil and criminal. There are no RIC to bring cases to my courts, and if any civil cases were brought, there is no body to execute our warrants or enforce our decrees. I did not therefore consider that any useful purpose would be served by attempting to acquire a courthouse for a court which cannot function and to arrange for the rent thereof to be paid by a local authority which won't pay it.[41]

The County Court judges gallantly tried to persuade the public to support their local court by stressing that they were now sitting under the authority of the Provisional Government as declared in the Proclamation, but few appeared in them to defend civil claims or oppose awards for malicious damage being levied on the rates. A judge in County Meath issued a public plea to urban and rural councils to instruct their law agents to resist these claims, adding by way of inducement that the Farmers' Union in Sligo had done so and thus succeeded in getting £150,000 knocked off their rates.[42] Yet when Judge Cusack responded to an IRA threat by adjourning his court, the Listowel solicitors were furious with him.[43] The failure of the government to speak out on behalf of the statutory courts – except on the lines of bland pronouncements that 'all courts were now Irish courts' – must have been bitterly felt,[44] but even more the fact that no steps were taken to encourage local bodies to return to them. After all, William Cosgrave was Minister for Local Government, yet prosecutions by Dublin Corporation alone in Parish and District Courts numbered several hundred.[45] Some Petty Sessions and County Courts did manage to hold sittings, although they were badly attended; however, few venues may have achieved the record of Limerick city, where on 8 April 1922, a local newspaper had reports of five different courts on the same page – the Parish Court, the District Court, Petty Sessions, Limerick Quarter Sessions and the Dáil Land Commission Court: moreover, they all appear to have sat in the same hospitable courthouse![46]

While matters of public health, sanitation or rates might be discounted as idiosyncratic to councils, the prosecution of its citizens for criminal offences and any loss of liberty that follows must be the concern of the State. It was here that the most obvious consolidation of the Dáil Courts occurred. Minor offences had long been disposed of at parish level, and while serious crime was dealt with by the Circuit Courts, some of the judges were unhappy with the absence of juries, and felt that it was fundamentally wrong to try a person for an indictable offence without a jury. Creed Meredith was particularly concerned, and Arthur Clery, who, it will be remembered, was a professor of law, put forward the novel idea that a panel of lay justices should sit with the trial judge instead of a jury.[47] However, Creed Meredith had his way, and an instrument was drafted containing eleven clauses and called 'Juries Decree 1922'.[48] There was no mechanism whereby the Provisional Government could have passed such a measure, but lists of jurors were drawn up and the idea was put into effect. The registrars were instructed that only petty juries were to be summoned.[49] There were reservations discernible among senior officials, but no one took any steps to halt the initiative, and by April criminal trials were taking place before judge and jury on all the circuits. The development attracted further publicity, and Meredith congratulated the large number of jurymen who turned up at the south Offaly sitting: 'It is right and proper that you should be associated with the Courts in the proper administration of justice. … Your presence here tends to stabilise conditions. … You come here readily and willingly to do what you can for the proper administration of law in the country'.[50] The Chief of Police reported to His Honour that four hundred cases had been heard over eighteen Parish Courts and two hundred disposed of in the District Court within the area. It is not to be wondered at that the people, reading regular reports in their newspapers, had reason to believe that these courts were the ones that had received government sanction and that the old courts were rapidly being phased out. When the IRA occupied the Four Courts shortly thereafter and prevented access to judges and staff of the established legal administration, it seemed scarcely possible that it could recover momentum: Commandant Rory O'Connor's remarks when asked about the inconvenience caused to litigants seemed to confirm this. In an interview given to the *Irish Times* he claimed that the County Courts were suppressed because they functioned under the Provisional Government and that he had stopped the High Court from that day.[51] The bitter irony was that he promised that he would safeguard the records, which he understood to be irreplaceable: his understanding did not prevent the destruction, under his command, of the Public Records Office two months later. The Lord Chief Justice, J.F. Molony, made arrangements to carry on the business of the courts in temporary accommodation at Dublin Castle and the King's Inns.[52] In the months that followed, he and his colleagues did not observe any lessening in the apparent support given to the Republican Courts by those now in power, nor in their acceptance by the public at large.

This was a time of great anxiety about whether or not the new state would ever take shape. Each step that was required to be taken by the Treaty was fraught with potential disaster, pushing the fragile hiatus, in which the factions held their breath, towards an explosion. While Collins, as head of government, searched for some accommodation with the republican ethos, he was being watched closely by the British in case he renege on his commitments to them. Eamon de Valera, on his side, had to balance his aptitude for consensus with the anger of the IRA, who had its own extreme wing to control.[53] Ahead lay the hurdles of the election, the constitution, the oath, the occupation of the Four Courts, and, overhanging all, the miasma of the fraught discontent in the North. It is understandable that the matter of courts should rank low in priority, all the more so if civil law and order was being maintained at some kind of acceptable level.

This necessary preoccupation with strategic and political issues was to lead the government to ignore individual rights and to betray the effort and cooperation which had been invested by ordinary people in pursuit of the nationalist dream. In fact, the minutes of government meetings and the memoranda passing between departments and advisers reflect little concern with popular reaction to the changed circumstances, and the vacuum was further deepened by the effective failure of the Dáil to meet during the most critical part of 1922. The Dáil Courts were, therefore, allowed to absorb criminal and civil jurisdiction over the citizenry without any thought being given to an overall policy, and no enquiries were being made about the legal realities that gave structure to everyday personal, civic and commercial relations.

6

Though the Heavens Fall

If the courts flourished out of the mind, if not quite out of the sight, of the Provisional Government, they were not immune from the partisanship of the Split, particularly its rapid escalation with the occupation of the Four Courts. Simon Donnelly, Chief of the Republican Police, raided one of the Home Affairs offices and carried off two typewriters and some documents.[1] He was immediately replaced by Peter Ennis, who passed on reports he received from his brigade officers of those court of officials who had been arrested by government troops for taking part in some disturbance.[2] Recruitment and training for the new police force, the Civic Guards, had begun, but it would be some months before they could take up duty,[3] so that the enforcement of court orders was still dependent on the volunteer police, whose loyalties, it can be assumed, considering the conduct of their former chief, were as confused as those of the general public; moreover, many of them joined the Guards. There is little evidence of any particular decision motivated by a bias on the question of the Treaty, but the certainties based on the integrity of the Dáil Courts were evaporating. It was no longer the climate in which a parish court clerk could express the bewilderment that Padraic O'Caorinn from Carrickderry, Co. Limerick, did in early February when asked to make a declaration of loyalty: 'I cannot for the life of me see how anything of a political tendency can hamper the operation of the Republican courts or in any way tamper with their efficiency. Whatever political view I hold shall be reserved, and not utilised to thwart or mar the efficiency of Dáil Eireann.'[4] There were incidents of IRA officers playing the role formerly reserved to inspectors of the Royal Irish Constabulary – that of interrupting court proceedings to determine their political hue. Cahir Davitt suffered a similar visitation in Kerry: the officer withdrew on being

told that it was a court of the Irish Republic,[5] the same unequivocal reply
the judge had given less than six months before to the same question posed
in different circumstances. He was also warned in a letter purporting to
come from a commandant in the IRA ordering him not to try a case
which was listed for hearing: it may well have been an empty threat, since
Davitt made immediately clear that he was taking orders from no one.
What disturbed him was that neither party turned up when the case was
called; it is one of the very few times in his recollections that he allows
an emotion to surface – in this instance, anger at the 'gross insolence
and contempt of Court'.[6] He recognised that if he were to make a judicial
order against the man, it was unlikely to be carried out.

It was not the first time that the absence of professional police
was deplored. In January, the Limerick City Registrar had advised the
Ministry that the Limerick Workers' Housing Association was preventing
the Volunteer Police from carrying out decrees for possession; 'until a
properly established paid police is formed, decrees of this nature cannot
be executed'.[7] With the coming of peace and the difficult symbiosis of
the military and the civil in the ranks of the Republican Police, it was
bound to have the effect of sands shifting underneath the courts, even
though they were still being extended. Without an impartial police force,
the judicial capacity to impose decisions by sanction would soon become
threadbare. However, in the meantime, there was no competition from
any other system. The Royal Irish Constabulary was being rapidly stood
down. The County Courts, whose work had been reduced by boycott to
nothing other than malicious in jury claims – which, in any case could no
longer be prosecuted until their fate, under the Treaty, was worked out[8]
– were adjourning such applications, and the Assizes had not gone out.
The enterprise of individuals in intimidating the former 'British courts'
appear to have been more a hawkish search for signs of contradiction
to the holy grail of pure Republicanism rather than the preoccupation
of its leaders. At Carrickmacross when the IRA prevented the Resident
Magistrate from entering the courthouse to hold the Petty Sessions, he
appealed to the local commandant; he was assured that the courthouse
would be available in the future.[9]

After the initial reaction to the proclamation of 16 July 1922, there
was no further threat to the predominance of the Dáil Courts, and with
the later occupation of the Four Courts, there must have seemed little

prospect that the previous legal establishment would long be maintained. It is beyond doubt that Republican officers engaged in the odd martial swagger towards both sets of courts – the same type had essayed a swagger in the pre-Treaty Dáil Courts[10] and here and there court officials were arrested for involvement in subversive activities,[11] but there is no hard evidence that the slide towards civil war affected the operation of the courts in particular, or that the intimidation of litigants in local disputes was of a more intensive nature than heretofore. It is worth stressing the generally routine work of the courts, right up to the outbreak of hostilities, since it was later maintained that disunity was already breaking them apart. It could equally be said that the hostilities themselves gave the government the opportunity to close the courts, since there was no further reason to preserve the visible structures of separatist policy.

On the political scene, the draft Constitution had been settled between the parties to the Treaty, which the majority had supported in the election on 16 June.[12] The arrival at these two milestones may have had something to do with the decision to reactivate the Assizes. The Provisional Government on 23 June authorised its Law Officer, Hugh Kennedy, to issue commissions to the judges for the Summer Assizes.[13] It was an extraordinary decision and it may have been only a straw in the wind because the same quandary as that in the abandoned Winter Assizes remained: where were the accused persons they would try or the body of cases they would hear? Once more the questions were to remain unanswered. Five days later, pushed by the tide of events, outside pressure and grim fate, government troops laid siege to the Four Courts and the Civil War began in earnest.[14] This time the Dáil Courts were not pushed to the bottom of the agenda: they appear in the cabinet minutes eleven times during the month of July.[15] On the 10th, the Law Officer and the Minister for Home Affairs were instructed to prepare a code for the courts in Ireland: this was most likely a signal that preparations were to be laid for the judicial administration provided for in the draft Constitution. It was also decided that 'the sittings of the Republican Courts were to be restricted as far as possible and ultimately stopped altogether'.[16]

A mass of contradictions belied the mild statement of intent and the implication that it would be a gradual process was deceptive. Three of the judges were already out on the Summer Circuit – Meredith in Carlow, Clery in Cork and Crowley in Kerry and Limerick. The *Irish*

Times, gallantly coping with the altered political circumstances where the rebels had replaced their natural masters, had already reported that the President of the Dáil Éireann Courts, Mr Justice Creed Meredith, had informed members of the Bar that the circuits were beginning from 22 June and that the Long Vacation would be from 7 August to 29 September, but a judge would be available in chambers during the period.[17] Nothing could be more *comme il faut,* judicially speaking. The list of towns where the sittings would be held had been published and three temporary judges had been alerted that their services would be needed because of the heavy lists. Nor is there any reference to impending changes in the correspondence files of the Ministry.[18] It is interesting that where it does appear is with the files of the Ministry for Home Affairs (later Department of Justice) which first became available in January 1991.[19] Nicholls had sent Upper Merrion Street, as requested, a list of the personnel in the Courts Section of the Dáil Ministry with a star against the names of those 'who were definitely known to be hostile'.[20] On the same day – 11 July – he wired each of the three judges outside Dublin that circuits were to cease on the orders of the Dáil cabinet and he was to return to Dublin. The operation was controlled from Upper Merrion Street and Nicholls's role as a cipher to convey government instructions was preserved for only a few weeks longer.[21] His name appeared at the bottom of a letter that Creed Meredith read out to a startled Supreme Court two days later. The court was exercising its original jurisdiction in the cases for hearing which were helpfully detailed by the *Irish Times* in its report the following day: many of them were bail applications. The most puzzling facet of the letter read out by Meredith was that it had not been addressed to him at all, but to Davitt, the more junior of the Circuit judges. It said:

> Pending reconstruction of the Judiciary the Dáil Eireann Cabinet considers it advisable that no further sittings of the Supreme Court should be held. Please see that this order is complied with.
>
> S. MacNiocaill
> Assistant Minister[22]

Within seconds counsel were on their feet asking what were they to do about their applications, but Meredith coldly replied that he had nothing to advise in view of the letter and he left the court with Davitt who had accompanied him; which, in itself, is puzzling because Judge Davitt was due to preside at a circuit sitting, which he did a short time later. The President may have wanted to underline his displeasure at the insult offered to his position by highlighting the blatancy of the executive interference in the courts and to distance himself from it. An emergency meeting of the Bar Council was called the following day,[23] and lawyers instructed in one matter frustrated by the *démarche* called at Upper Merrion Street to protest, which indicates that they at least appreciated that the action had moved from Dawson Street.[24]

Davitt's failure to discuss this dramatic episode in his memoir is disappointing. The month of July 1922 was full of incident and he himself was stricken with a bad bout of gastroenteritis during the latter part; so his confusion is understandable. He did recall presiding at the Dublin Circuit sittings on the same day[25] – 13 July – which was also reported in the newspaper. There is no explanation of why this court was unaffected by the ban on all Circuit Courts two days previously. It is possible that Davitt was made privy to the decision to close the courts shortly before his colleagues were, perhaps because it was felt that his sympathies were more in line with the status quo: if so, it was particularly unfair to him. He was due to go on circuit to the midlands the weekend following the attack on the Four Courts, but Leo McCauley, his registrar, was frustrated in his attempts to get cash at the bank or definite information on train departures because of the tense situation in Dublin, so they did not travel at all. Davitt got in touch with the local registrars and cancelled the courts in his area, presumably days before the Ministry ordered the rest of the courts to stop. Interestingly, the *Irish Times* reported on 11 July that Meredith had been unable to travel to Longford and 120 circuit court cases had been postponed indefinitely. This was obviously incorrect: Davitt was to take the Longford sittings and on 11 July Meredith was returning from Carlow to preside at the Supreme Court as scheduled.[26] It was Davitt also who sent a telegram to Clery suggesting that he and Crowley return to Dublin to discuss the position of the courts in the light of the outbreak of civil war. They both declined, but it would have been difficult to imagine that they continued to hear proceedings, since Nicholls also notified all District Registrars that sittings were suspended and they were to see that the order was obeyed.[27] An even more dramatic clash was about to occur between the judiciary and the government, and it is this clash that has historically been seen as the justification for the courts being suppressed, although it is clear that the government had already begun the process of disestablishment.

George Plunkett was a prisoner in Mountjoy Jail following the capture of the Four Courts. His father, Count Plunkett,[28] applied for a conditional order of habeas corpus for his release. The affadivit that he filed was overtly political, challenging the abandonment of the Republic and the legality of the Treaty,[29] but that in itself would not undermine the correctness of the procedure. The application was made to Crowley, who had been appointed a judge for life. He had not been dismissed from office and had inherent jurisdiction to hear it and make whatever order he considered appropriate. It was *ex parte* and he granted the conditional order usual in such circumstances, directing that the Minister for Defence and the Governor of Mountjoy show cause, that is to justify the prisoner's detention within seven days. The government had a complete answer to any application in a civil court on the question of Plunkett's detention, regardless of any extraneous matters like the validity of the Treaty: he was a military prisoner and outside the court's jurisdiction. After the Four Courts surrender, it had been promised in respect of the captured men that 'until such time as their cases can be individually examined, the Government is prepared to treat the prisoners as military captives, and to allow them, consistent with public safety, privileges not accorded to ordinary prisoners.'[30] Moreover, the application was in line with others that had been heard by the Supreme Court or by a single judge, and notice of conditional orders had been served on commanding officers of military camps around the country.[31] At a date as recent as 27 June 1922 an order of attachment was made against Commandant Patrick Powell at Ballinrobe Camp because he had failed to produce one James Morris to the court having been ordered to do so. He was given one last opportunity to purge his contempt but since the Registrar did not know whether Powell was with the Regular Army or the Republican Executive forces, he took the precaution of sending a solemn warning to Commandant General Rory O'Connor as the officer commanding the Four Courts that 'extreme measures would be taken and that he should be aware of the responsibility he was incurring in not complying with the court order.'[32] O'Connor would have received the letter on the same day that government troops began the bombardment of his garrison. Powell may have been among the officers there because there was a pattern of the Army cooperating with conditional orders, certainly to the extent of explaining the circumstances of the applicant's arrest or the arrangements for his trial. Undoubtedly, the different reaction to the particular application of Plunkett was the stance taken by his father and those behind him, notably Eamon de Valera and Austin Stack. Refinements of the law[33] were considered inappropriate to meet a challenge to State authority at the hour when the very survival of the independence so hardly won was hanging in the balance. Nevertheless, from another direction came a plea for the rule of law. James Creed Meredith had a meeting with the Home Affairs Minister to discuss the current situation in regard to the courts and he was evidently dissatisfied at the outcome, because, in a letter written from his holiday home in Skerries, he referred to the cabinet decision to suspend the Supreme Court and his interpretation that it was necessary in order to prevent further litigation being initiated which might delay the transfer of business when the judiciary was reconstructed. However, he wanted the Minister to confirm that the Vacation Judge would still be sitting to hear urgent applications:

> As you are aware applications for writs of Habeas Corpus have already been entertained by us on many occasions. On the last occasion, only a few weeks ago, Mr Power appeared on behalf of the State. As our jurisdiction in the matter has been repeatedly recognised and never questioned, and as the Habeas Corpus could only be suspended by a Decree of the Dáil, it is clear that any of the judges who, on instructions from the Executive, were to refuse to entertain an application would, besides exposing himself to the severest penalties, be guilty of a constitutionally indefensible act. As to applications to admit prisoners to bail – a matter also affecting the liberty of the subject – the seriousness of refusing to entertain such applications is equally obvious.[34]

The next day Meredith was given his answer: it was 25 July and the day before the detention of the prisoner, George Plunkett, was expected to be defended in court. The cabinet decided that 'the Minister for Home Affairs should rescind the Decree creating Republican Courts except

Parish and District Courts outside the City of Dublin'.[35] That there should
be no doubt at whom this particular edict was directed, a copy of the
Minister's Order (presumably made immediately) and stated to be with
the concurrence of Dáil Éireann was delivered by messenger to Crowley
late that night.[36] The following morning Crowley made the conditional
order absolute when nobody appeared on behalf of the Minister for
Defence or the Governor of Mountjoy, and he issued orders for their
arrest. The report of the proceedings in the *Freeman's Journal* was marked
'not passed' by the Official Censor,[37] and the attention of Michael Collins,
the Commander-in-Chief, was directed on 2 August to the matter of
the warrant Crowley had issued.[38] The following notice appeared in *Iris
Oifigiúil* on 1 August:

DÁIL EIREANN

THE Aire um Gnothaí Duitche with the concurrence of the Cabinet
of Dáil Eireann hereby decrees that the decree of the Aire um Gnothaí
Duitche purporting to establish courts of law and equity and criminal
jurisdiction as part of the government of the Irish Republic be and
the same is hereby rescinded and declared to be of no effect as from
this date save to the extent to which the said decree was or may have
been effective to establish Parish Courts and District Courts outside
the city of Dublin.

Dated this 25th day of July 1922
E.S. O'Dugain, Aire um Gnothaí Duitche.[39]

It is difficult to escape the conclusion that the notice was so worded in
order to mislead. Dáil Éireann had no part in the unhappy exercise,[40]
and in any case, the new Dáil, which had been elected in June, had not
met.[41] The decree that established the courts in June 1920 was passed
by the Dáil, not by the Minister for Home Affairs (Aire um Gnothaí
Duitche) but somehow it had been decided that they had been set up
by the previous ministry without authority: the gloss also allowed
for the current Minister to close them.[42] Had the courts been closed
everywhere, there would have been no summary jurisdiction since the
Petty Sessions had virtually ceased. However, the Metropolitan Police

Court still functioned in Dublin and the Parish and District Courts in the country were excluded from the ukase to continue until some alternative could be planned.[43] It must have been hoped that the public would not notice the absurdity of an Irish court being legal in Dromcollogher, or even Aughnacloy, but not in Fairview. People did not have to wait for the official publication to learn that their government had made radical changes in the administration of the law without the sanction of the legislature. A statement had been issued on the day the Supreme Court was suspended which went to considerable length to stress that the Dáil Courts were originally established to provide an acceptable alternative to those which were functioning under the British government, but these were now in Irish hands and there was no longer any need to have two systems.[44] It was a waste of money paying for a complete judicial system which was not being utilised and which had criminal, licensing, lunacy and other jurisdictional powers which the other courts lacked. The tone was brisk and practical, with no hint of nostalgia for the fairly recent days when the same courts were being extolled as the showpiece of Irish self-sufficiency. Even more striking is the absence of reference to a characteristic which was being heavily promoted elsewhere – their essential 'illegality'.[45] Suddenly the basis on which the courts had been founded – to usurp those established by statute – was being turned about in order to obliterate them.

Ernest Blythe had recently been appointed Assistant Home Affairs Minister.[46] He drafted a memorandum on local courts in which he forecast that an Act would be necessary to legalise the decisions of 'the Sinn Fein Courts' and that the new judicial system, which would be established under the Constitution, would not be in operation before June 1923. Once the Supreme and Circuit Courts were gone, it meant that the lower courts would also have to go, since there could be no appeals nor could prisoners be sent forward for trial. 'The fact that these courts are illegal cannot long be concealed.'[47] There was no explanation of how this conclusion was arrived at, but it was a theme shortly taken up by the Law Adviser and repeated as fact in correspondence for a brief period, and then as inexplicably dropped. Blythe goes on to consider how to provide for summary justice during the interregnum. Since the Resident Magistrates were all to be pensioned off, the Petty Sessions would lapse. 'We would then have one system with nothing higher than parish courts,

another system with nothing lower than County Courts.' The solution to
the dilemma would be the temporary appointment of legal men of sound
national views as Resident Magistrates but to call them District Justices.
This was to be the recommended policy, although 'it may be advisable to
consult Parliament before taking definite steps.'

Hugh Kennedy drafted a letter for the Minister to send to Meredith
and Davitt. 'As you are aware the Ministry is of the opinion that the
late Minister's decree purporting to establish Courts was wholly illegal
and not authorised by the Dáil Decree. The effect of that is that all the
decisions of the Courts in the past two years are open to challenge and
that prisoners sentenced are entitled to apply for writs of habeas corpus
and secure their release as persons unlawfully held in custody.'[48] It was
necessary to quieten the anxiety caused by 'their questionable authority';
there was a strong possibility that the recipients might be sued for
presiding over such unstable tribunals, and therefore their cooperation
was solicited to help the Ministry in assessing the numbers of prisoners
and in framing indemnity proposals. A minor curiosity is that the two
men were addressed as judges in a letter that tells them that their courts
were a sham, which must have presupposed that their appointment by
an egregious minister was a nullity. It is salutary to recall that this letter
had already been drafted when Meredith was expressing to Duggan his
concern that the courts remain the guardian of civil liberties. The same
dangers presumably lurked for Clery and Crowley, but no one wrote to
warn them, nor the Land Judges, O'Shiel and Maguire, the standing of
whose courts does not seem to have troubled anyone. One irony, among
so many, is that the only court challenge to the legality of the courts which
had operated under the authority of the First Dáil was made against the
Land Judges and within a few months. While the Judges of the King's
Bench found as a fact that Maguire and O'Shiel were presiding over an
illegal tribunal,[49] they also found in law that they could take no judicial
notice of non-statutory bodies: the plaintiffs did not even get their costs![50]

If it was hoped that the abrupt loss of access to justice would be
soothed away by reassurances about money saved or the doubts raised
on its lawful status, the authorities were to be disappointed. There were
no other courts in any state of readiness to replace them, in spite of the
bland emphasis on the comprehensive range of judicial services to hand.
The statutory legal establishment was camping out in Dublin Castle and

the King's Inns, the Four Courts was a smouldering shell and the Petty Sessions had faded away. Nothing had come of the earlier mention that the Assize Judges should go out, and it was not possible for them to travel in the present circumstances. It was very late for Blythe to be weighing up the options: neither did he consider that the government's decision might not be accepted as a *fait accompli*. Gavan Duffy, the Dáil Foreign Minister and a signatory of the Treaty, resigned in protest.[51] Paul Vignoles, one of the court organisers, wrote about the resentment felt by people in the West who had been proud of 'the Republican Courts as being the first Courts established by them'.[52]

The same anger that greeted the statement about the courts in January surfaced again: it seemed that the judicial administration which they had been assiduously advised to shun was now being promoted and praised by the former advisers.[53] Some of the fears might have been eased if the public had been told that the hated Resident Magistrates were not being brought back, but those gentlemen themselves had not yet been told. The proposal that professionally qualified men might replace lay judges in the District Courts had been made before, but not followed up;[54] the government having exerted itself to close the Dáil Courts was bereft of a planned alternative. Kennedy replied to an enquiry from a solicitor: 'It is hoped a new magisterial system of a satisfactory kind will be constituted at an early date'.[55] However, nothing better illustrates the cul-de-sac into which the government had led itself through panic than the communication addressed to it by its chairman on the day it purported to rescind the Dáil Decree of 29 June 1920. Michael Collins wrote from his headquarters at Beggars Bush Barracks: 'What will be the procedure for bringing men to trial before a Civil Court and what Civil Courts are there to bring them before?'[56]

Had the question been posed to the Dublin justices, they would have had no difficulty providing the answer. A meeting was called of the North Dublin District Court on 11 August 1922 to consider its position and a statement was issued. It was stressed that the courts had been established by Dáil Éireann which had not rescinded the decree: 'Until the recently elected Dáil has had the opportunity of deciding the question, the Justices agree to hold the Courts as usual'.[57] They did so, but in conditions reminiscent of a former regime. The police who came to spy and report back to the authorities were in the service of the native government.[58] This happened during a brief, but surprisingly vindictive, period. A journalist from the *Freeman's Journal* waited upon Kennedy to inform him of the happenings in the Dublin North District Court when the Corporation's law agent had called attention to the official notice that the decree establishing the courts had been rescinded. When he was directed to continue with whatever application he was making or face contempt charges, the journalist advised the judges not to make fools of themselves and proceeded to the Law Officer to tell him all.[59] The Chief of Police reported that he had 'raided' the Dublin District Court and found among those present T.V. Cleary, the Supreme Court Registrar, and Michael Noyk, the solicitor.[60] When Cleary returned to his office, he was immediately fired. Noyk's legal talents were often engaged by official departments but now the Army was advised that he had been observed at a subversive court: the fact of Cleary's dismissal for similar misconduct was pointedly referred to.[61] Crowley, the doughty judge who had the temerity to issue warrants for the arrest of a minister and a prison governor, was snatched from the street one night and incarcerated in Wellington Barracks for about ten days. He was in the unhappy position of being able to compare prison conditions then with those on the last occasion he had been arrested for presiding at a Dáil Court. He wrote to Gavan Duffy, 'I have never recovered from the effects of the 13 months I spent in jail before, and I am afraid this will ruin my health altogether.'[62]

Davitt received a letter from Crowley, addressed to 'C. Davitt Esq. Judge of the Supreme Court', although he must have known that Cahir Davitt had been made Judge Advocate General early in August. Kennedy had recommended him for the position and Michael Collins was intent that he was to take up the post without delay.[63] In fact, he continued to be paid as a Dáil Court judge instead of by the Army until it got around to noticing the discrepancy almost a year later.[64] Davitt felt it was unjust to punish Crowley for carrying out his judicial duty as he saw it, and he made representations to Richard Mulcahy who was now the Commander-in-Chief and ironically the person whose arrest Crowley had ordered on 26 July. Mulcahy, who had probably no part in what had happened to Crowley, directed the Adjudant General to investigate the matter because he thought that it could lead to bad publicity. The President of the Executive Council, William Cosgrave, was unsympathetic when it was raised in the Dáil by Gavan Duffy; in fact, he treated it with a pronounced skittishness.[65] The

Dáil, which had been elected in mid-July, had finally met on 9 September so that at least there was now an elected forum where the representatives of the people would have an opportunity to discover what arrangements were in hand to provide for their constituents' legal requirements.

7

Justice in Transition

The Third Dáil – or from the the British view of the Treaty, the Provisional Parliament of Southern Ireland – met at Leinster House on 9 September 1922.[1] None of the thirty-five anti-Treaty deputies, except Larry Ginnell, attended. William Cosgrave, who had been elected President of the Council of Ministers, signalled the closing of shutters on the Sinn Féin experiment when he said, 'Dual government, you may take it, ends from today.'[2] Of the two cabinets approved by Dáil Éireann at the start of the year, Arthur Griffith and Michael Collins were dead, and Gavan Duffy had resigned. The remainder including some former ministers, like Blythe, who had been outside the Provisional cabinet, formed the Executive Council with Duggan and Finian Lynch as Ministers without Portfolio. Kevin O'Higgins was Vice-President of the Council and kept his post as Minister for Home Affairs. When the matter was raised in a later debate, he spoke briefly and rather dismissively of the Dáil Courts but promised that at least some of those who had worked in them would be provided for in the new order.[3] A committee would be reporting on how the work of the courts would be wound up, and paid magistrates had been put in place as a temporary measure until a judicial system was formally established.

The committee to which he referred[4] had been brought together on foot of the letter which Duggan, the former minister, had sent to Meredith and Davitt on 28 July and, as we know, had been drafted by the Law Adviser six days earlier. It appears that there was a conference between the Assistant Minister – whether Blythe or Nicholls is not specified – and James Creed Meredith on 8 and 9 August, following which the latter prepared a lengthy memorandum in which he examined the jurisdiction of the Parish and District Courts outside Dublin.[5] He also submitted proposals on ways in which the Dáil Court decisions could be validated by legislation or could, on application, be made a rule of court. His assumption was that the reconstruction of the court system was imminent. He urged the adoption of the latter method; since it was confined to the necessities of each case, it would eliminate the need for registration, which would require investigation, and it would have the added benefit of encouraging people to recognise the new courts. The following month he drafted a decree[6] which would have empowered the Minister for Home Affairs to appoint both stipendiary and honorary magistrates to take over the Petty Sessions jurisdiction. The existing High Court and County Courts could receive any final decree or order of the Parish and District Courts as if it were a judgement by consent and make it a rule of court. In addition, the Minister would appoint not more that six judicial commissioners to wind up the business of the Dáil Courts and finally dispose of all proceedings. Henry O'Friel, the Secretary at the Ministry, wrote to Hugh Kennedy urging that a committee be set up at once to consider the question, and he recommended that the Minister would issue 'a Decree as per draft enclosed'[7] simultaneously with an announcement that the committee was at work. In the event, no decree was issued, but Meredith chaired a committee consisting of George Nicholls, B.J. Goff, the solicitor who had acted as a temporary circuit judge, and himself, with Padraic Crump as secretary. Their report, delivered on 11 October, proposed the establishment of a judicial commission whose work would include registering the judgements made by the Dáil Courts, ruling on any questions of evidence that arose out of this task and hearing outstanding appeals.[8] Matters at hearing in the lower courts were to be abandoned: those before the Circuit Court could be prosecuted only by special leave. Surprisingly, in spite of the fundamental illegality of the courts which had been so stressed in the letter forming its terms of reference, the committee felt that decrees, particularly for rates and damages, should be enforced immediately and that prisoners 'serving well-merited sentences' be kept in custody. It was an extraordinary recommendation for lawyers to make and suggests that the issue of illegality, recently considered central to the abolition of the courts, was not taken seriously by the members: Meredith was later to show publicly that he did not accept it at all. They did accept, however, the government's intention to validate the decrees and to indemnify the judges, but that would have to await a legislative Act. Moreover, the jurisdiction of the members of the proposed commission was to flow from the original Dáil Decree establishing the courts in the first place, 'for it is the Departmental Decree setting up the Parish and District Courts that was rescinded'. To call this disingenuous is to overstrain the language. There was only one decree setting up the courts of justice and of equity, and the Ministry was authorised to bring in criminal courts when appropriate.[9] All the courts were put in place at the same time as the constitution contained in the *Judiciary* clearly sets out, and the Parish and Circuit Courts were given criminal jurisdiction from the start:

> The Aire Um Gnothaí Duitche having been authorised by Dáil Eireann to establish Courts of Law and Equity and Criminal Jurisdiction as part of the Government of the Irish Republic hereby decrees that there is to be established:
>
> 1. A Supreme Court sitting in Dublin and having jurisdiction over the Republic.
> 2. District Courts having jurisdiction in their respective Districts; and having special sittings called 'Circuit Sittings' presided over by a Circuit Judge.
> 3. Parish Courts having jurisdiction in their respective Parishes.[10]

Limits of their respective jurisdiction in civil and criminal matters were set out in the following pages. The committee was put in the awkward position of having to square the judicial powers with which it proposed to invest the commissioners with the undoubted hurdle that the Decree of 29 June 1920 had been revoked, and moreover, they had to find a way to allow the slightly dubious process of law to be brought to a conclusion without an enabling Act. The majority of District and Parish Courts were still in existence: the Dublin justices would have still maintained that they all were! In fairness to its members' common sense, the committee may have been signalling to the authorities that it was accepting the closure of the courts as *de facto* but that the *de jure* facility of Dáil Éireann to confer jurisdiction remained until that body itself decided to the contrary. So the rationale was that the Commissioners would stand in direct succession to the original judges – in fact, it was earnestly urged that they should, as far as possible, be the same men – and that they would have the same authority as the former Supreme Court and hear all proceedings awaiting judgement in that court. The number of cases was thought to be more than seventy and they estimated that it would require the work of four commissioners over three months. District Judicial Commissioners would deal with outstanding matters in the lower courts: between six and eight of them should dispose of this work on a circuit basis. It was accepted that there could be no legislative basis at the present time – until the Constitution had been enacted, no bills could be introduced in the Dáil – but it was understood that, when all was completed, legislation must be passed which would validate not only the decisions of the Dáil Courts but also of the Commissioners-to-be, and at the same time indemnify all concerned against any claims for wrongdoing.

A short time after the draft report had been presented to the Executive Council, Meredith wrote to Kennedy in a panic.[11] A prisoner sentenced by the Dáil Courts was about to apply to the Lord Chief Justice for a writ of habeas corpus, and he would be successful unless the Court was to hold that all the powers and machinery of the Dáil had vested *pro tem* in the Provisional Government together with those bestowed by Article 17 of the Treaty – the functions of government transferred from the British administration of Ireland – otherwise 'not only the Dáil Courts but all are involved in the taint of illegality – Civic Guards, IRA, Dáil Decrees etc', and it would be inadvisable to set up the Commission until this point of jurisdiction had been settled. It was a very late start for this hare, particularly by the chairman of a committee who had just presented a report which had discussed the question of jurisdiction with considerable subtlety.

However, it seems a relatively simple question had been overlooked and had just struck Meredith. From where would the Minister get his power to meddle in the remnants of the Dáil administration since duality no longer existed and he could be regarded as in succession to Austin Stack, Eamonn Duggan and Kevin O'Higgins only if the Provisional Government was the lawful successor to the Dáil? The symbiotic arrangement had been going on for a long time, and it is impossible to understand why Meredith should treat it as if it were a novelty. Kennedy, to whom the matter was now being referred, had advised as early as 14 December 1921 that the purpose of the Provisional Government was administration only and Griffith and Collins had underlined its separateness from the Dáil from early on, as we have seen. All the functions relating to the administration of the law which were transferred were specifically set out in the statement of 18 January and later in the Articles of Agreement;[12] as might be expected, the Dáil Courts did not feature.

It appears from Meredith's letter that the kernel of the matter rested on whether the Lord Chief Justice was going to release the prisoner by finding that his custody was unlawful.[13] It was ludicrous to imagine he could come to any other decision or that he would take a substantially different view than he was to take in *Kelly* v. *Maguire* and *O'Shiel* within a few months.[14] Not only could it be expected that a statutory court would refuse to recognise a usurper, but Kennedy himself had already advised by way of the letter of 28 July 1922, which he had drafted for the Minister, that all such prisoners were being held illegally.[15] In any case, it was policy to release a prisoner who challenged his custody and his Lordship was not likely to be troubled with such weighty political matters as the extent of executive powers.[16] The likely sequel to Meredith's *crise de nerfs* is that the plan to appoint a commission without benefit of statute was abandoned – at least, it does not surface again until it is in the form of a draft Bill. Having already cast doubt on the judicial proceedings of one administration, it was probably considered unwise to risk undermining the very basis of the commission before it was even in place. The result was that discontent and uncertainty in legal matters deepened and the Ministry was forced to suffer a great deal of pressure from the solicitors and the public because of the paralysis. Those who tried to move their affairs forward by taking them to the courts which had been advertised as now in native hands, suffered disapproval and protests,[17] not only by their opponents but also from public officials who were caught up by the hiatus and were forced to mediate between both parties demanding satisfaction.

The most pressing need was to have some form of summary justice uniform throughout, particularly since the difficulties that had beset the formation of the Civic Guards had been resolved.[18] Twenty-seven legal gentlemen, a little more than one half of whom were solicitors, the rest barristers, were appointed to be Magistrates by the Constabulary (Ireland) Act 1836, although they were never publicly called anything but District Justices.[19] There was no further need to preserve the local

Dáil jurisdiction, and on 30 October 1922 the Dáil decree establishing native courts was rescinded in respect of the lower courts outside the city of Dublin.[20] The new justices began to sit in the areas assigned to them, and within a short time it was apparent that, in a year when the administration of justice in Ireland had received an unfair amount of body-blows, the arrival of the District Justices to the towns and villages did much to restore confidence and continuity in due process. It is not to the credit of the Executive Council, which had neither the time nor the interest to give much thought to the men it appointed, beyond being satisfied that they had some legal qualification and that they harboured no dangerous yearning for a republic; the good news was in the character of the individuals who had to provide a bridge between the statutory and non-statutory courts, which had only barely gone, and the social contract of the new state, which had not yet achieved a form.[21] It did not help that violence and murder were still being waged around the citizens,[22] that no Rules of Court were even in the process of being drafted, or that there were no effective procedures for the trial of serious crime. Nevertheless, the justices brought commitment, courage and adaptability to their task: they were generous in their praise of the Dáil Courts and were concerned to make the transition period as unremarkable as possible.[23] Reports of court proceedings in the provincial press reflect a more or less unchanging pattern of summary jurisdiction; just as there was little real difference in the reports of Petty Sessions and those of Parish Courts in the days when they had appeared side by side.[24]

If the Ministry for Home Affairs felt that the immediate problem of the current local administration of justice had been solved, it was not being allowed much peace by litigants frustrated by the uncertainty into which their claims had been cast.[25] All kinds of ruses were resorted to in an effort to placate them: arbitration was privately arranged,[26] the sheriff was persuaded to hold back on the execution of decrees,[27] and people were discouraged from bringing fresh proceedings in the only courts now available to them. Henry O'Friel,[28] the Secretary of the department, had served as a Dáil judge and had a great deal of sympathy for those people who had secured a judgement in a case where both sides had been represented and now had to endure their opponent either ignoring the matter altogether or re-litigating the dispute in another court. Two cousins named Collins in County Limerick were the opposing parties in an action that seemed set to rival Jarndyce and Jarndyce, the case immortalised by Dickens in *Bleak House*.

There was a dispute about the ownership of two fields which had been mortgaged in the previous generation. East Limerick District Court in December 1920 had given a judgement in favour of John, who had immediately been put in possession by the Volunteers, in spite of his cousin Matthew Collins indicating that he intended to appeal.[29] Local feeling seems to have been on the side of John, but Stack rightly felt bound to intervene as the Minister responsible and to insist that the *status quo* be restored until the appeal was heard. It came before Judge Davitt in the autumn of 1921 and he gave judgement to Matthew, but the Supreme Court reversed that decision on a case stated shortly before its shutters were pulled down. Matthew, who was still in hard-won possession, entered proceedings in the Chancery Division of the High Court of Southern Ireland to restrain his cousin from trespassing in the land, whereupon John's solicitor, Hugh O'Brien Moran, bombarded the Ministry with righteous indignation:

> It would be a calamity if it [the Chancery Division of the High Court] was to be permitted to exercise a jurisdiction by way of review or otherwise over Decrees and Orders made by the Supreme (Final) Court of Dáil Eireann at a time when these Courts were recognised as Final and Binding on all parties and particularly on all parties who appeared to and availed of the Jurisdiction without Protest.[30]

While it is a rather typical overstatement of a case by a partisan lawyer, nevertheless it remains an accurate enough description of the position that his client, and the clients of many other solicitors, found themselves in at the time. Nor were fractious litigants and their solicitors the only backwash of the Dáil Courts with which O'Friel had to contend among his other duties: it should not be forgotten that he was the closest official and personal adviser to the minister responsible for public order in a State torn by civil war. Solicitors who had prosecuted for the State in the Circuit Courts complained that they had not been paid and the young men who have acted as registrars to the professional judges sent in well-documented claims on the sudden cutting off of their expected earnings by the closure of the courts.[31]

The repercussions of the Collins case will be recounted shortly, but before the letter was received, some official effort was being made to relieve the stasis of Dáil Court orders and decrees, although it promised far more than it could possibly deliver. It may either have been intended to divert the grievances into a show of doing something positive to help or the first genuine step to prevent a further degeneration into total confusion – or, more likely, a combination of both. A notice appeared in the national press on 23 February 1923 inviting persons who had obtained a decree or order from a Dáil Court to apply to the Ministry to have it registered.[32] A complicated bureaucracy was erected around the applications that were to be made. The applicant had to swear out his claim before a Commissioner for Oaths. A form was to be completed in respect of each person affected by the decree with a stamped addressed envelope, and all dispatched to the Ministry with the application. Twenty-one days were given in which to comply and this time was further extended on two dates in March and April, which tends to suggest that the primary purpose was to find out the numbers involved. In fact, no registration was attempted beyond giving the applications a number and putting them in pigeon holes: by April they numbered over five thousand.[33] Only the more fortunate litigants would have a court order recognisable as such; the majority would have had to rely on other documentary evidence, such as a notice from a clerk or perhaps an entry in a solicitor's account book. Those affected by the decree were notified on the form that they had fourteen days in which to object on stated grounds; otherwise, the decree would be registered. When the objections were returned, there was an obvious stalemate because there was no forum to resolve the argument. As might be expected, many respondents declared that they objected to registration, if only for the reason that they did not want orders executed against them. Moreover, the public announcements released a flood of enquiries from solicitors about the matters still pending or about appeals that had not been reached. They were told that they would be dealt with later, but that the more urgent work was the registration of unexecuted decrees.[34] No one seems to have asked in what form they were going to be registered or how they would be enforced. The failure to use the information now available on the volume and kind of litigation that had to be brought to a conclusion was responsible to a large degree for the inefficient working of the Commission when it was finally set up.

A draft Bill had been prepared by mid-April with Meredith in the role of consultant.[35] It provided for three Judicial Commissioners, who would have the same powers as a judge of Saorstát Éireann and could hear all matters which pertained to the Dáil Courts, whether they had been at trial or only set down. They would be given the power to direct a particular matter to another court to be decided or to remove it from another court into theirs. A judgement given by them could be appealed only if the Attorney General certified that there had been a grave miscarriage of justice. A decree would first have to be registered in the proposed registry before it could be enforced. It was intended to set up a fund under the joint control of the Secretaries for Home Affairs and Finance from which litigants could be refunded deposits or compensation paid for work done on behalf of the Dáil Courts. The Act would be called the Dáil Éireann (Enforcement of Decrees) Act 1923. A fundamental difference of approach from that of the Committee's report in the previous October[36] was the opening up of all Dáil Court proceedings to the Commission and not merely those that had already begun or had been appealed. What was startling, however, was the proposed power to interfere, almost at will, in the workings of other courts: an issue could be sent to another court to be heard, but when decided, that decision would be considered to have been made by the Commission. The Commission judges could prevent a case being lawfully decided in any court on the grounds of it being prejudicial to their jurisdiction. There was no precedent for such proposals, particularly in a temporary body to be created to deal with the detritus of tribunals which had only recently been found illegal by the High Court of Saorstát Éireann.[37]

From the beginning, the cost of the Commission was the cause of endless bad-tempered rows between the senior officials of the Ministry of Home Affairs (shortly to be renamed the Department of Justice)[38] and those in Finance. O'Friel, whose particular project it became, shrewdly played down the sums when it was at draft stage, saying that the total cost would not amount to over £6,000 and that its work would be finished in a year.[39] The request to the public to send in applications for registration had at least given a more realistic view of the job that lay ahead. He suggested a salary of £1,200 for the Chief Commissioner and £1,000 for the others, but once the Commission was safely in place, he held that nothing less than £2,000 and £1,500 was in keeping with the dignity of their office. Officials in the Ministry of Finance were openly scornful of what they considered a pretentious and flagrantly expensive undertaking. It is impossible not to have some sympathy with them because they had to find funding for several other temporary commissions at the same time.[40] It is equally impossible not to admire O'Friel's adroitness in procuring what he had determined to be proper recognition of the *magisterium* of the Dáil Courts.

The bickering with the officials at Finance lasted a long time,[41] but there was also the occasional joust with the Attorney General, as Kennedy now was, and with the Parliamentary Draftsman. The latter objected to the insertion of an indemnity in the Bill on the grounds that 'such a clause would suggest that the Dáil Courts were illegal tribunals'. Matheson, the Draftsman, complained that he had also been instructed that the draft should be amended to allow cases to be reheard where a party had stayed away from the British courts from patriotic motives.[42] Understandably, he had difficulty converting such expressions into legal language. Two weeks before the Bill was to be introduced, he felt that radical additions were being urged on him by Home Affairs. Matheson's bewilderment is understandable: judgements which were obtained against defendants who absented themselves from the established courts on principle had no specific connection with legislation to clear up the proceedings of the Dáil Courts, although there had been a strong relationship between the setting up of the new courts and the boycotting of the old ones at the time. However, those who had obeyed the direction of the Dáil had been repeatedly promised by the Minister's officials that the Act would give them the opportunity to have their cases reopened. Another provision the Draftsman had been asked to make at the last moment was that where there was a time limit in which an action could be brought – from 18 December 1918 to 21 July 1921; the limitation would not apply to proceedings brought within three months of the passing of the legislation.[43] This was plainly outside the ambit of the Dáil Courts since they were no longer in existence: it could apply only to those who had prosecuted no claim in any court during the period. Matheson was clearly so unhappy with such a mixed bag of innovative law that he would not proceed on his own: these additions were 'not of such a nature as could be considered by a Draughtsman without express instructions'.[44]

Kevin O'Higgins introduced the Bill in the Dáil on 19 July 1923 and, although the debate which followed was passionate and personal, it was confined to a few deputies.[45] The vast majrotiy of those present must have had some involvement in the Dáil Courts during the years just gone by, yet they made no contribution. Darrell Figgis had been a justice and had been one of those who had drafted the constitution, but he spoke only once.[46] George Nicholls did not speak at all in spite of being the Assistant Minister in charge for seven months. Tom Johnson, the Labour Party leader, made several practical observations and regretted the passing of lay tribunals rooted in the community.[47] It was left to George Gavan Duffy to pay tribute to the courage and dedication of those who had brought 'the British system of justice to a standstill', and called the decision to close the courts panic-stricken.[48]

O'Higgins launched an extraordinary attack on the courts: he called them channels of corruption and abuse, which had done some good work for a very short period during the summer of 1920 in providing a rough and unlearned settlement of minor disputes, but were incapable of administering anything in the nature of strict law. They had served a purpose when the RIC had withdrawn to barracks and there were no Petty Sessions. After the Truce, they had lost their 'purity' and had also allowed applicants to obstruct justice by granting injunctions against proceedings being brought in the established courts.[49] Apart from the fact that this was Sinn Féin police, the Minister must have known that an injunction is an equitable relief[50] and therefore could properly have been granted only by a few well-known persons: Meredith, the *éminence grise* of O'Higgins' own department and the Chief-Commissioner Designate, Arthur Clery, Professor of Law at University College Dublin, Cahir Davitt, then Judge-Advocate General and Diarmuid Crowley, all the professional judges to whom matters of equity were reserved under the constitution of the courts. Not only was an unpleasant shock awaiting them on reading about themselves in the paper the next morning, but also for the parish priests, farmers, doctors, businessmen, trade union officials and other leaders of the community who had served as justices. The more O'Higgins was challenged on the facts, the more irrational and vindictive he became. It is difficult to understand why he could not have made a brief and graceful reference to the work of the Dáil Courts and got on with the substance of the Bill – whose purpose, after all, was to absorb, register and execute the judgements of those he affected to despise and transfer them into the High Court. It may be that his animosity towards Gavan Duffy rendered him irrational, or that the hurried and undemocratic suppression of the courts touched a raw nerve still.[51]

He was not prepared to be any less acerbic to the urgings of Deputy Gerald Fitzgibbon that to allow any party to bring proceedings when the time limit had long passed would cause legal chaos. Property that had been distributed to heirs, or land bought or personal injury claims not pursued for years were all to be put to the hazard of unscrupulous claimants who had not bothered to prosecute their case for six years or more. The deputy stressed that the provision had nothing to do with the Dáil Courts. It is highly improbable that he had ever attended one. Gerald Fitzgibbon was the representative for Dublin University, a King's Counsel and son of a former Lord Justice of Appeal.[52] His interest in the Bill was only this section and the potential damage it threatened to established law. O'Higgins insisted that he had received requests from commercial men for such a provision since they had refrained from going into any court during disturbed times because they saw little point to it.[53] He would not accept that it would 'authorise people to promote dead and gone causes again'. He also refused to reconsider allowing a defendant who had ignored proceedings in an 'enemy court' to apply for a retrial, although this facility had been promised. Evidently other pressure was brought to bear because, in the closing days of the debate, the Executive decided that a right of appeal should be inserted for 'persons who abstained from defending cases in the so-called British courts during the Anglo-Irish struggle'.[54] Not only was a government amendment to this effect brought in, but O'Higgins also accepted one that would exempt bona fide land transactions from coming within the section which suspended the time limit on proceedings,[55] which Fitzgibbon had urged on him as a minimal safeguard. Having spent most of the debate furiously opposing both amendments and using the opportunity to lambaste the aims and ethos of the Dáil judicature, he suddenly conceded them – albeit with the bluster that they were not of great significance. In this placatory mood, he also allowed an amendment of Gavan Duffy's which was of far more importance to the substance of the Bill; its omission in the draft was a serious lapse.[56] It allowed any decree of a Dáil Court, once registered, to be pleaded in future proceedings as *res judicata,* that is, as a matter already decided. As the Bill stood, this could only have been done by prior application to the Commissioners; only Gavan Duffy noticed that it would have nullified the long-term purpose of registration because when the Commission came to an end, a party to an action would have been deprived of the opportunity to prove a prior judgement.[57]

Preparations for the commissioning – out of the Commission head -quarters had already been put in hand by O'Friel.[58] In the internecine scramble for a foothold in Dublin Castle, so recently vacated by another administration, he had succeeded in reserving the prime site of the former guardhouse in the Upper Yard.[59] Philip McQuaid, a solicitor from Newry and friend of William Cosgrave, was to be the Registrar; the two clerks who had been in charge of the abortive registration of decrees had already moved in with the files. There was never a question as to who would be Chief Judicial Commissioner: James Creed Meredith was the obvious candidate.[60] He had been the President of the Supreme Court and chairman of the committee whose proposals had resulted in the Act which created the office. It was left to him to suggest his junior colleagues, the Assistant (or Puisne) Judicial Commissioners. They were St Lawrence Devitt and Diarmuid Crowley. It could scarcely have been without trepidation that the latter was approached – perhaps there was a faint hope that he might refuse – but the preference had been for former judges.[61] Davitt was already in public office, as was Kevin O'Shiel.[62] Conor Maguire would have been unsympathetic and, in any event, had only recently been called to the Bar.[63] Arthur Clery had retreated to academic life and remained steadfastly aloof from any further association with judicial preferment.[64] Fears that Crowley might be a slow-burning fuse were to be justified and even his appointment by the Governor General was delayed, at his request, because he wanted to get de Valera's approval first.[65] The Act passed into law on 9 August 1923, the Commissioners held their first court on 21 August, and not much later they were complaining that not enough cases had been prepared for them to hear.[66] During the two years of the Commission's existence, this was the recurrent complaint. The administration of the Registry, whose job was to process applications for the registration of decrees, notify the parties on record and, where there was an objection, list the case for hearing, was quickly bogged down by its own procedures.

Philip McQuaid may have been honest and hard-working, but he was unfit to be Registrar.[67] Not only was he indecisive and incompetent, but he had an exaggerated idea of the importance of his office. This led him to conclude that he had 'a judicial decision' to make in respect of each and every application and that it was a duty which could not be delegated. The experience of Crump, O'Toole and T. Gordon Flanagan of the Dáil Courts Section, all of whom had been transferred to the Commission, was wasted in peripheral tasks, instead of doing the actual registration.[68] A decree or court order was first to be registered before the other parties were notified who could then object to its registration, in which case the whole dispute was heard from the beginning by the Commissioners. An applicant had also the right to appeal against the Registrar's refusal to register his judgement. Applications that had come in response to the public notice of the previous spring were to be treated as having been made under the Act, but McQuaid insisted that they be made on a new regulatory form, instead of taking steps to ensure that both forms of application were compatible.[69] He devised all kinds of circulars and questionnaires to elicit information that was already in the files. Solicitors were frequently written to for information which had already been given, and, by November, they were circularised that they must arrange for their town agents to call at the Commission's office since the Registrar was too busy to enter into correspondence.

It was not alone McQuaid's obsession with empire – building and printed forms that put pressure on O'Friel to defend the Commission: he was also forced to fight for what he considered was the minimum level of salary that should be paid to the Commissioners commensurate with their high office. When he was unable to rattle the obduracy of the mandarins at Finance, he enlisted the help of his own Minister:

> It is important to the prestige of the Government that the Dáil Courts should be buried with honour and that no person would be able to say that the same Government which is paying High Court Judges £3,500, County Court Judges £1,600 and District Judges £1,000, considers £1,200 good enough for a puisne Judge and £1,500 for a Presiding Judge, if it is only a question of seeing that justice is done to people who supported the Dáil Courts.[70]

McQuaid wrote to O'Higgins on 24 August 1923. The Attorney General had weighed in on the side of Finance, fearful that anything might disturb the salary scale for the new judiciary then in the planning stage.[71] The Secretary and his assistant, Stephen Roche, proceeded to dissect his comparisons, and when Kennedy found that his private opinion had been disclosed to Meredith, O'Higgins was forced to apologise. O'Friel persisted, however, and the letter written by Ernest Blythe's private secretary embodies his department's impatience with what it saw as the pretensions of the Commission, as well, perhaps, as Blythe's unaltered opinion of the Dáil Courts:

> In Mr Blythe's opinion the true view is to consider the Commissioners as, more or less, engaged in clearing away a mass of dead debris: for the purpose of this definite and limited task, they exercise an extensive jurisdiction but the occasional exercise of such jurisdiction in the course of their work in clearing away this mass, cannot fairly be taken as putting them on the same level as Judges of the High Court.[72]

The private secretary happened to be Leo McAuley, who had been registrar to Cahir Davitt a mere sixteen months before. He might have explained to his master that a decision of any court can hardly he dead as long as it remains unchallenged, apart from the implied dismissal of a litigant's proper interest. What Blythe failed to understand was that the jurisdiction vested in the Commissioners was higher not merely than that of the current High Court level, but of any other court then or in the future. They had been given power to remove from any court any matter they considered, in their unfettered discretion, to be of concern to the Commission: their decisions were beyond appeal in any court of law, nor could another court remove a case from their jurisdiction by an order of *certiorari*.[73] In other words, whatever they decided, quite simply was. Never before or since has an Irish court been given such unlimited powers. This was rehabilitation of the Dáil Courts on a grand scale indeed.

Moreover, a compromise was agreed about the salaries in which the levels sought were achieved by way of bonus.[74] In the meantime an opportunity was given to the judges to assert the *magisterium* of their court and to reassert the authority of the Dáil Courts. *Collins and Collins* was given yet another judicial airing and more than assured its place in Irish legal history by becoming the only written judgement of the

Judicial Commissioners that has survived.[75] John Collins's solicitor had been persuaded to avail of the opportunity to register his judgement in April 1923 by way of delaying the proceedings being taken in Chancery by his cousin Matthew. The latter's solicitor, in turn, was advised that he could appeal against the Supreme Court to the Commissioners when the Dáil Courts (Winding-up) Act was passed.[76] Accordingly, an application for leave to appeal by the defendant in *Collins and Collins* was the first case listed for the court, although it was not heard until 2 November. Meredith, who delivered judgement on 7 November, said that the judges wanted to set out the principles by which they would be guided.[77] Leave to appeal was refused because the matter had already been decided in a final court of appeal, which had been of as 'competent a jurisdiction'[78] as the one in which the defendant had attempted to have the issue re-litigated – the High Court. The Chief Commissioner, with considerable judicial elegance, defended the Dáil Courts against O'Higgins's bitter attack in the debate; although he never once alluded to it, the connection is unmistakable. The facts of this particular case were heaven sent, for here was a litigant who had done the very thing that had so exercised the Minister in the Dáil – taken his case to one court in order to thwart the judgement of another. But in this instance, the defendant had gone to the statutory court to frustrate the lawful findings of a Dáil Court. The Chief Commissioner said that the Act under which they were now operating had made the Dáil Courts' decrees enforceable and had 'completely sanctioned and approved' the policy on granting unjunctions.[79] Matthew Collins had very little merit on his side, unless one believes there should be an endless prospect of appeals, but neither did he merit the six pages on the subject of his application that were devoted to injunctions, since he had not applied for any and neither had his opponent.[80] It is impossible to avoid the conclusion that the Commissioners were stung by the denigration of the courts which O'Higgins had chosen to mount on the weak ground of injunctions and they had seized on the first chance publicly to set the record straight.

Having done so, they were ready to set out on circuit to take the appeals and re-trials of the lower courts.[81] Each was accompanied by his registrar[82] and travelled in some comfort and with the local Garda superintendent alerted to his arrival. Their activities were regularly reported in the papers, frequently under the heading of 'Dáil Courts', which was as correct a description as any other of the work they were doing. Not only can one find reference to a case that originally appeared in a news report some time in the past, but cases with a local background which were heard before a full Court in Dublin were also reported. There were no compelling reasons to give written judgements, since the Commission, temporary and *sui generis* in its limits, could not set judicial precedents, which reinforces the impression of a sub-agenda in *Collins and Collins*. Another report[83] that catches the eye is a short item which says that *In re Plunkett* – the case which is often seen as the *cause célèbre* in the opening stages of the Civil War – had come up for mention and was adjourned. Crowley, never a man for agonising reappraisals, was barely out on circuit when he was again issuing writs of habeas corpus to the Commander-in-Chief, the same old adversary, General Mulcahy, this time to produce witnesses who were being held in the Curragh.[84] One such internee, Robert de Courcy, the mayor of Limerick, was brought in custody to give evidence in a case: the losing party had to pay six guineas for the cost of his military escort![85] Once the first circuit was over, it had impinged on solicitors and their clients that legal affairs so long in limbo could now be moved and concluded. In spite of all the preparation and the publicity, many solicitors[86] professed to have been caught unawares and found it cumbersome that the procedure had changed from that of the old Dáil Courts because the duty of notifying clients of the hearing of their cause fell on them rather than on the District Registrar – who no longer existed, in fact. Another oversight was that the last day on which application for registration could take place was 25 October 1923, and partly because of the confusion between the public notices in the spring and those in August, an extraordinary amount of applications were made after the due date. A legal fiction was invented to include them in matters pending, in other words, that they were cases being heard at the time of closure: this led to the list being clogged with what were really applications to register. Meredith became worried and complained that there were about 300 cases in the same position.[87] The simple remedy of having the Minister extend the time by Order was not considered: the problem remained to be added to the unmoving mountain in the Registry.

O'Friel was rapidly losing patience: his department was being dragged into every facet of the Commission's operation on a daily basis.

He was forced to prop up McQuaid's uncertain grasp of the work which remained undone and whose response to every communication was to demand more staff. He declared that he badly needed a legally qualified assistant, a court registrar with his assistant and two legal clerks, adding that the immediate appointment of the first three was a priority.[88] This coincided with Meredith's complaint that the judges were not being given enough work to fill their lists. The report submitted on 13 November showed that only 129 decrees had been registered, three months after the Act had been passed.[89] O'Friel was so desperate that he appealed to Meredith early in the New Year: 'The Registrar has three Law Clerks, three junior officers, a retired law clerk as paper-keeper and two typists, but registration does not seem to reach twenty per day.'[90] The Ministry of Finance kept sniping at his heels for estimates of how much longer would the Commission have to be maintained and how much more was it going to cost. The reply was always the same: provision of extra staff would prepare much more work for the Commissioners to process, and it was their high salaries (for which the writer had fought tooth and nail) which was the biggest cost: therefore more staff would result in less expense in the long run and a quicker end to the Commission.

By November 1924 it was clear that no end was in sight and it was accepted that it would not be possible to wind up the Commission and simply transfer the records to the new High Court which had been established, along with the other courts of the Irish Free State the previous June.[91] There was also the question of judgements which would, of their very nature, continue to require legal effect such as perpetual injunctions or the administration of estates.[92] The solution was to move the Dáil Courts section as an ongoing jurisdiction into the High Court. What was to be done about the unfinished registration had not been decided when a startling discovery was made by John O'Byrne, then Attorney General, on a visit to the Commission's office in January 1925. He found that in about 4,000 cases 'registration was notional rather than real', consisting of a reference to a file entered on a folio: he was adamant that incomplete records could not be handed over and the corrective work must be put in hand at once.[93] There was a flurry of activity to get sanction from Finance to engage extra staff and, after two weeks of negotiation at a very high level, permission was given to pay the existing staff a shilling for every registration completed outside office hours.[94] Within a month a total of

3,000 decisions had been registered. This unusual efficiency probably owed as much to the last Commissioner, Charles Stewart Kenny, having been asked to supervise the work, as it did to the financial incentive.[95]

It goes without saying that the Commissioners always had the more congenial side of the work to do. They had only to hear the arguments and deliver their findings. Their registrars looked after the paperwork, they responded with dignity to the status of the role accorded to a judge and they had an assured income to a level they might not have earned at the Bar.[96] But more than any other advantage, they had prospects. There was the near-certainty of judicial office in the courts of the new state. James Creed Meredith, who was later to become a Supreme Court judge, was deservedly among the first judges of the High Court: about the same time, St Lawrence Devitt became a Circuit judge. Charles Wyse Power, who had been co-opted as a fourth commissioner in October 1924, was appointed Chief Judicial Commissioner in place of Meredith, whereupon Crowley resigned in chagrin. He would make his mark in the High Court, but as a plaintiff, not as a judge.[97] William Kenny and Eugene Sheehy were the new appointments: both of them became judges, as did Wyse Power.[98] It was fair enough reward for the abandonment of their careers at a critical juncture, for they were all young men, and most of them had served in the national army. For the final few months there was only one Commissioner left. The Dáil Éireann Courts (Winding-up) Act 1925 became operative on 1 May 1925. Crump was transferred to the Chancery Court, but O'Toole and Dunne were transferred along with the Commission records and those of the Dáil Courts to the jurisdiction of the High Court[99] whose judges were invested with the functions and powers of the former Commissioners, as well as their immunity from appeal. The function and authority of the Dáil Courts finally merged with those created by the first native government. This was the vision of Arthur Griffith and Sinn Féin in the thrust for an independent Ireland that had existed since the Act of Union.

There was a final and fitting grace-note at the close. Matters remained to be heard in Clare, the county which was the first to give substance to Griffith's dream. The last time the Commission went out on circuit, it did so in the person of Mr Justice Meredith of the High Court, who set out on 23 July 1925 to adjudicate in proceedings that had come before the local Dáil Courts in 1921. But even in the Banner County, judicial events had telescoped somewhat and this interesting footnote to legal history merited only a small paragraph in the local paper under the heading 'Sinn Fein Courts'. The rest of the paper was filled with detailed and vivid accounts of District Courts from Sixmilebridge to Corofin, from Kildysart to Killaloe. Most of the goings-on seemed a far cry from Griffith's reasonable and satisfactory settlement of disputes, but in so far as anyone can make such a claim, its final form was perhaps better suited to the public weal.[100]

8

By Law Established

The sudden decision to close down the Dáil Courts was contemporaneous with a direction to the Minister for Home Affairs and the Law Officer 'to prepare a code for Courts in Ireland'.[1] There is little indication that any thought had been given to the important issue of how a legal system would evolve from the sparse enough commitment in the draft constitution.[2] It was reasonable to assume that there would not be any startling innovation in the law itself, given that the members of the King's Inns and of the Incorporated Law Society were long trained in the common law of England, and even the revolutionary courts had not sought to dent that tradition. Nevertheless, a new hierarchy of courts would have to be planned, and a judicial establishment created. There were a great number of appointments to be filled – always an exciting prospect both for the patrons and the hopeful candidates. The public could not be expected to welcome the reinstatement of His Majesty's judges. It must have therefore come as something of a shock that the person chosen to be the chairman of the committee, whose members were 'to consider and report' on an Irish judicial blueprint, was none other than Lord Glenavy,[3] who had previously been the Lord Chief Justice and, later, Lord Chancellor. Apart from two solicitors and two barristers, the remaining members of the Judiciary Committee, as it was called, were evenly balanced between the representatives of the *ancien régime* and the new dispensation.[4] The only other element deemed necessary to leaven the stolid consistency of lawyers was a commercial interest and thus Declan Howard, the President of the Chamber of Commerce, was added to their number on Meredith's advice.[5] No one suggested that there might be a voice for social reform, but neither was there, as might have been in later years, a mandatory clerical presence. It would be untrue say that it was axiomatic that there was no woman appointed; after all, women had played a visible part in the national movement; what was more pertinent, perhaps, was the lack of female lawyers or female business owners to represent those interests primarily assumed to be concerned with the construction of legal systems.

In a letter addressed to the committee on 29 January 1923, William Cosgrave wrote:

> In the long struggle for the right to rule in our own Country, there has been no sphere of the administration lately ended which impressed itself on the minds of our people as a standing monument of an alien government more than the system, the machinery and the administration of law and justice which supplanted in comparatively modern times the laws and institutions till then a part of the living national organism. The body of laws and the system of judicature so imposed upon this Nation were English (not even British) in their seed, English in their growth, English in their vitality. Their nomenclature were only to be understood by the student of the history of the people of Southern Britain. A remarkable and characteristic product of the genius of that people, the manner of their administration prevented them from striking root in the fertile soil of this Nation. Thus it comes that there is nothing more prized among our newly won liberties than the liberty to constitute a system of judiciary and an administration of law and justice according to the dictates of our own needs and after a pattern of our own designing. This liberty is established and the headline is set in the Constitution drawn up and passed by the elected representatives of our people.[6]

Hugh Kennedy had already asked Serjeant Hanna, a leading barrister, to gather information on other administrations through his Bar Council contacts in Australia, Scotland, the United States and New Zealand. He had also solicited the help of Professor McNeill to 'jot down any thoughts that might occur' to him about the functions of judges, advocates and legal functionaries derived from the ancient law tracts of Ireland.[7]

County councils, traders' and farmers' associations were publicly invited to make recommendations to increase efficiency and economy in legal administration and court procedure. As was to be expected, individuals or bodies all had a particular axe to grind. Daniel Blayney, recently returned from South Africa, enclosed the Transvaal Resident Magistrates' Court Ordinances. The Listowel solicitors felt it unfair that remuneration for the services of a skilled profession should be based on the amount of a claim and not on the work involved. The barristers were anxious that the centralisation in Dublin would be maintained and that the two branches of the profession would not be amalgamated. The Cork Traders' Protection Association proposed that court registrars would give creditor-plaintiffs telephone notice that their case was going to be called in five minutes. Lord Justice O'Connor urged the desirability of judges being highly paid and surrounded by great ceremony, 'as the populace are impressed by pomp and show of power'.[8]

Only the unsolicited submissions made by women's groups were wholly disinterested and, without exception, they pleaded for the non-criminalisation of children. One of the groups, the Children's Care Committee, not only sought and got an interview with Kennedy in the person of its secretary, Ethel McNachtan, but submitted its own advanced scheme for child courts and obtained through a Paris correspondent, Dr Merrill, information on the juvenile courts which were then operating in Canada.[9] Another group urged that where a young person had got into trouble because of youthful propensity or curiosity, the record should not follow him into adulthood – a reform still being urged today. The Irish Labour Party and Trade Union Congress presented its 'Skeleton Suggestions for Legal Reform', and while the outline predictably referred to Workmen's Compensation and the law in the first sentence, it set out a concise structure for a court hierarchy which managed without too much legal verbiage to include civil, criminal and land jurisdiction, as well as an appeal procedure, from summary courts to a Supreme Court.[10] In an addendum, it recommended that judges' salaries should be free of income tax – a claim that was also made in relation to their own salaries as Dáil judges by both Davitt and Crowley, and appears to have been finally conceded to them.[11]

Practical ideas were put forward by two men who were shortly to be appointed among the first District Judges, Louis Walsh and Bartholomew J. Goff. The latter was a member of the Winding-up Committee and the former of the Judiciary Committee, although both these distinctions were in the future when they offered advice. In fact, Walsh and Kennedy renewed a student acquaintance on the basis of a letter the former had written to the *Freeman's Journal* as early as 20 July 1922. A few days later he took up the matter of local courts enthusiastically, warning that it was vital to demonstrate a clear departure from their previous character. British terms should be abandoned: 'Apart from the necessity of Irishing them, you know what slaves of words we are in this country, as the rubbish that has been talked since the 7th Decr. shows. For instance, if you are appointing professional minor Justices, don't call them "R.M.s" or you will damn the whole system. Call them "leasbreithimh" or something …'[12] Walsh thought that some of the existing Parish and District Judges should be chosen to sit with a professional lawyer in Petty Sessions (under a different name) which 'must be as expeditious and convenient as the Dáil Parish and District Courts'. Goff also took the view that there were lessons to be learned from the Dáil Courts, experience:

> In general I would recommend the retention, very largely at any rate, of the Republican system with, of course, some important necessary modifications. Notwithstanding its many shortcomings from a system hastily organised in order to meet an emergency, the system has on the whole, and particularly as far as the Lower Courts are concerned, justified its existence and given satisfaction. It has, too, to a greater or lesser degree, woven itself into the scheme of things and taken on a popular character. To reject it, therefore, *in toto* would hardly be diplomatic and might give rise to dissatisfaction among the people in general.[13]

He was in favour of Parish Courts and District Courts maintaining the same territorial jurisdiction and of 'honorary Justices' assisting a stipendiary magistrate in Parish Courts. The warning against returning to the British pattern expressed by both Walsh and Goff was echoed in a letter sent to George Nicholls by Paul Vignoles on the same day – 26 August. He was the organiser of the Dáil Courts in Sligo, Mayo and Roscommon, and he felt it his 'bounden duty' to say that everywhere he went in his area, people who were government supporters were fearful that it was the intention to return 'to the Courts they at one time sought to destroy'. He felt that anything other than courts based on the Republican system, with certain basic improvements, would greatly damage public confidence in the government; 'the people would gladly welcome a reorganization of these Republican Courts in a manner that would secure of them adjudicating from men of legal knowledge and experience assisted by Lay-representitives [*sic*] chosen by the people themselves'.[14]

A preliminary conference of the Committee was held at Government Buildings on 2 February 1923; the final report was submitted to cabinet on 17 May. A great deal was accomplished between those dates, most of it channelled through the office of the Attorney General, with whom Michael Smithwick, Secretary to the Committee, corresponded.[15] The presence of James Creed Meredith ensured that the practical experience of working as a judge outside the judicial establishment gave him a different perspective on the problems and delays caused by impractical procedures. While acknowledging that the present task was one of reconstructing the judiciary rather than changing fundamental law, he thought the opportunity should be seized to remove the dead hand of regressive precedent as much as possible and to simplify appeal procedures. In the first of a series of memoranda and letters on 28 August 1922 he said that the experience of the Republican Courts 'during the last nine months' (which can be taken to refer to the time he sat as a Circuit judge outside Dublin) had shown that many cases were not taken to a hearing because of the expense and the delay involved.[16] It is clear that a consensus soon evolved that the County Courts[17] were a waste of resources, so that the Circuit Courts in the Dáil scheme, which had a criminal, civil and appellate jurisdiction, became the model to replace the Quarter Sessions, County Court and the Assizes – with considerable modification. An outline of the Committee's recommendations was approved at its meeting on 23 April 1923 and the final draft was sent to President Cosgrave via Smithwick shortly before 17 May.[18] The report was published by the Stationery Office at a price of 1s. 6d. At least some of the work of drafting the Courts of Justice Bill on the basis of the very detailed report was given to Arthur C. Meredith KC,[19] probably because Arthur Matheson, the lone Parliamentary Draftsman, was inundated with work at this time, not least the contentious matter of draft legislation to wind up the Dáil Courts.[20] Both Cosgrave and Kennedy were extraordinarily optimistic about the length of time it would take to have the Judiciary Bill passed: the Attorney told a sheriff that 'it would be law before 7 August';[21] Cosgrave informed Kennedy that he had been assured that it would be passed before the Dáil rose for the summer recess.[22] Their calculations were out by almost a year.

As soon as the Dáil Courts Winding-Up Act was passed, the Courts of Justice Bill was introduced. In an opening statement on the same day, 31 July 1923, Cosgrave made what he thought was an ingratiating appeal to the deputies: 'I feel and know that if the subject matter with which I am attempting to deal were in more capable hands all the concessions which I crave would be willingly assented to.' He wrote the propaganda against the British administration of justice which had been the cornerstone of separatist doctrine: 'The Bench in Ireland had the most distinguished and able jurists and conscientious lawgivers so the Bill endeavoured to regulate the necessary alterations with as little disturbance and as free from offence as was possible under the circumstances.' Such sentiments were unusual, to say the least, coming from the head of a government put in power by a combination of armed conflict and civil disobedience. It was a crude attempt to persuade the House that no great changes were involved so 'that all the concessions would be willingly assented to.'[23] His listeners were not particularly impressed because there was a general election in a few weeks and the Second Reading was not reached when the Dáil was dissolved on 9 August 1923.[24]

The Bill had, therefore, to be introduced again on 20 September 1923, and Cosgrave told the Dáil that its most notable feature, apart from the District Justices' Courts, which 'have been in existence for some time and have given considerable satisfaction', was the proposed scheme for Circuit Courts; it had been borrowed from the system set up under the First and Second Dáil.[25] They would replace the existing County Courts and most of the present day-to-day jurisdiction of the High Court which was locally centred. They would differ from the 'old British circuit system' in that adequate time would be allowed for cases to be properly heard. Most claims to the value of £300 would be heard in these regional courts; it would mean that parties would no longer have to travel to the High Court in Dublin for actions involving anything over £100. This apparently modest extension of the jurisdiction of the former County Courts raised a storm of protest from a handful of deputies which went on through several sitting days in which the House was constantly warned of the legal Armageddon that would follow from Circuit judges forever traversing the country, *sans* books, *sans* the latest reports, and above all, *sans* the

collective wisdom of the Law Library in its physical manifestation. The
chorus of outraged sensibilities was led by Captain William Redmond and
Professor William Magennis – 'Deputies Cox and Box', as Tom Johnson
described them.[26] It is hard to exaggerate the unflagging opposition
to a proposal whose purpose was to effect increased efficiency and a
considerable reduction in costs. Redmond put forward an amendment
to lower the limit to £100 which was the current level in the County
Courts. He harangued the deputies on the evils that would follow from
such a radical departure – decentralisation, local Bars, and the dread
that it might lead to the amalgamation of the two professions. When his
amendment was defeated, Professor Magennis proposed that the limit
should be £200 – and the same arguments were put again. The unabashed
clientelism is startling by modern practice: for example, Magennis was
allowed to introduce a proposal on behalf of the Bar Council.[27]

It was evident from the beginning that any attempt, however
innocuous, to harness the independence of the judges was going to be
discerned and opposed, not only by those deputies who made no secret
that they represented the Bar of Ireland and not their constituents in
general, but by the Labour interest as well as by several independents.
At High Court level, it was centred on the issue of mode of dress and
of address: the robes to be worn or judicial titles were matters for the
Bar and Bench to decide, without even the *nihil obstat* of the Minister.
Neither would the Executive be allowed to intervene in the Circuit
Court by means of deciding the Rules of Court or when an individual
judge would retire. However, over the institution of the District Court
the vigiliance of parliament never allowed its eye to blink. The folk-
memory of the Resident Magistrate – civil servant and chief constable
– forever at the bidding of government, permeated the resolve that he
would never be allowed to return under another guise. Magennis put it
bluntly: 'Now Castle government is gone, let us make sure that it has gone
with a vengeance and that it cannot return under another name.[28] Every
clause and subsection of the proposals relevant to the administration of
summary justice was examined and challenged, in both the Dáil and the
Seanad. Cosgrave, in particular, was to find that he had talked himself
into a trap. In his rash effort to rush the Bill through without debate, he
had continually referred to its being merely the reflection of the Judiciary
Committee's report. Deputies were able to point out that in no place in

the report was there provision 'to include the Minister in any rule making authority for any court – District, Circuit, High'.[29] Furthermore, were the Justices to be paid with money provided by the Oireachtas rather than from the Central Fund, it would mean a debate on the Estimates in due course. The chance that any decision of a particular justice might, as a result, become a matter for debate and censure was felt to be undesirable by all the deputies who spoke: Cosgrave's attempts to gloss over the role of the Executive and stress the benefits of parliamentary supervision – 'parliament is entitled to certain safeguards ... at any rate the power to review such rules as would be made'[30] failed to move them.

The deputies were indefatigable in their determination that the judges of the lowest court – 'the poor man's court' – should have the conditions of their appointment on the same footing as the other courts and that no residual control, no matter how slight, should remain with the government, the chief minister of which was considerably taken aback by the unremitting opposition. Lawyers, academics and the Labour Party were united, probably as never again: amendment after amendment was brought in and one that went to a vote was defeated by a margin as low as fifteen.[31] Another, moved by Redmond, was simply to substitute the exact words of the much-vaunted Judiciary Report for those in the corresponding section of the Bill.[32]

Every issue that might surface in court, such as school attendance, bad debt, title cases, children's prosecutions, was a matter of lively and well-informed discussion. The questions were lobbied fittingly – at the Attorney General, who had been elected to the Dáil in the August election: within a year, he would be at the apex of the structures whose framework he was being called upon to defend, singlehandedly, since Kevin O'Higgins, the Minister responsible, was absent for most of the debates. Other Chief Justices have been former members of the Dáil since then, but none has had the major role in devising the system over which he would, in time, preside. Kennedy, accustomed to having his advice heeded by ministers and civil servants, was exposed to immediate challenges on his view of things. Tom Johnson proposed the insertion of a section which would provide for a pre-hearing of a civil dispute by a District Justice, with the consent of the parties, in an effort to have the matter settled by conciliation. It was a sensible suggestion and would not have prejudiced anyone's right to a formal hearing. Kennedy dismissed it out of hand on the grounds that such procedures were desirable only where there was a rigid codified system and, in any case, it would not work.[33] He may not have been surprised that, for once, the lawyers agreed with him and Johnson, bowing to the Attorney General's superior knowledge, withdrew his proposal.[34]

When on 16 January 1924 the Bill was moved in Seanad Éireann, Sir Thomas Esmonde invited Lord Glenavy to vacate the chair so that he could give his fellow senators the benefit of his views as chairman of the Judiciary Committee. He took the opportunity to deplore the departure from their recommendation, evident in the Bill, in matters of the proposed ministerial role in the Rules of Court and in deciding the all-important question of wigs-and-gowns.[35] A piece which appeared in the *Sunday Times* on 20 January 1924 accurately forecast the progress of the Bill when it declared that many of the amendments that had been steadily fought for in the Dáil would be carried in the Seanad. The writer said that President Cosgrave had thought in September that he was going to put it through the Dáil in three days and through the Seanad in less, but 'the delay has effected this gain, that public interest in the principles and problems it raises has now been aroused. The process of conflict and delay is proving to be a process of national education and that is a great gain'.[36] Glenavy, who confessed to feeling himself to be 'a sort of father to this Bill',[37] led the unwearying opposition to any intervention by the Executive on a continuing basis in the regulation of judges.

The District Court became the fulcrum of the debate, as it had in the Dáil. Kevin O'Higgins was again absent and, initially, Cosgrave was alone in defending the legislation and protesting the innocence of any intent to retain the power to bring recalcitrant justices to heel. A sympathetic Seanad brought in a special Standing Order to allow the Attorney General, who was not a Minister, to participate in its proceedings.[38] Kennedy's position was undoubtedly difficult; he had been at the centre of the committee on whose unanimous report the Bill was supposed to have been drafted, so he was persistently and eloquently challenged on the departures from its recommendations. Not only that, but Article 64 of the Constitution guaranteed the independence of judges, and the admission that District Justices were also judges under the Constitution had been reluctantly wrenched from the Attorney General in the Dáil.[39] Several amendments were proposed and then the government struck back, provoking what Sir Thomas Esmonde rightly called 'a constitutional crisis':[40] it challenged the right of Seanad Éireann to pass an amendment that justices were to be paid from the Central Fund and not by a vote on the Estimate – the same amendment which had failed in the Dáil. The argument was on the lines that the Governor General had in September 1923 made the appropriate Order, which was a financial measure, that the Dáil had passed it and the Seanad could not overturn that arrangement. A special committee composed of Senators Glenavy, Douglas, Brown and O'Farrell met over a period of two weeks to consider 'the most important question to come before the Seanad in reference to its powers'.[41] Their report vindicated the Seanad's right to pass the particular amendment, as might have been expected, but in any case, it was rejected by the Dáil together with only one other – that the title 'Judge' be substituted for 'Justice' (a change that took a further sixty-seven years to be accepted).[42] However, forty-two amendments were accepted, as the prescient *Sunday Times* correspondent had forecast. Not only that, but the compromise which Glenavy had urged in February – that the justices' salary should become a charge on the Central Fund after the passage of some years – was brought in by a government amendment to the Section. The Seanad made no secret of its sense of achievement when it passed the Bill on 3 April 1924.[43]

It was a lesson in parliamentary democracy for the government, which had perhaps become unused to the idea of checks and balances in its first nine months of being subject only to the Treaty. Cosgrave's performance was particularly inept. He genuinely believed that this complicated and important legislation – and moreover one on which everyone might be expected to have strong opinions, whether in Parliament or without – could be pushed through on a nod. The original miscalculation was compounded by the nonchalant attitude that the strongly felt concerns voiced by members of both Houses of the Oireachtas could be met by cajolery or a slippery refusal to face the issue of judicial independence over months of discussion. His insistence that the proposed restraints on the judiciary would give Parliament the chance of scrutiny rang hollow in the face of his failure to acknowledge that it was that precise facility it was exercising in questioning the legislation before it was embodied in the law. After all, these were the elected representatives – whether of the people in the Dáil or of particular interests in the Seanad – and it was embarrassingly facile for the President to maintain, as he did, that there had been an election since the Bill's circulation (almost immediately, in fact) and that the public had had 'the opportunity of considering it in every single phrase, in every single Section'. He added that no one had assaulted him, or said the proposals were too expensive or contrary to the Constitution. Cosgrave threatened to take the Bill to a plebiscite or else that it would be held up for 270 days in the Seanad. 'I have been obsessed from reading in the Press for some time past an extraordinary disposition to belittle, to reduce, the status of the executive Council of the State and its officers in every possible way'.[44] He was teetering on a dangerous denigration of Parliament in this particular outburst and could not have considered the import of his words. A former revolutionary should have been proud of the standard of debate and measured comment that came from the elected assembly of which he was the apex and which was only in the early stage of its existence. Once the Courts of Justice Act had been passed and the Civil War over, Cosgrave guided the State into calmer waters and regained a proper perspective of democracy in action.[45]

While the lawyer-legislators may have dominated the debate in both Houses of the Oireachtas and were prominent – although not alone – in nailing down the independence of the judiciary at every level, they were not victorious in having all the provisions accord with their interest. Although they were allowed to read openly from briefs prepared by the Bar Council and the Incorporated Law Society, they did not succeed in diminishing the status of the Circuit Court.[46] If the long passage of the Bill had lessons for the Executive, it should also have alerted the legal establishment that there were other voices to be heard in matters of courts and the administration of justice: other people who were articulate and knowledgeable and not to be excluded by experts talking above their heads. The regular reporting of the happenings in both Houses over a six-month period informed the public of the changes which would order their legal affairs in the future and the back-and-forth arguments about seeming detail opened windows on the mechanism by which these changes would be effected. There could not have been any doubt that whatever system of courts was eventually set up, it would be difficult to claim that any person had been unaware of the changes that were planned. Given the fate that had unexpectedly overcome the courts set up by the First Dáil, it was fitting that, this time around, the public had received an amplitude of advance information, even if the government had not planned it that way.

Equally unplanned was the fact that the District Courts had already been in existence for almost two years before their formal establishment. The Justices had been appointed as an emergency measure to fill the dangerous vacuum created by the abolition of the Parish Courts and the Resident Magistrates, which had foolishly been allowed to coincide.[47] Their mission, according to one of their number, 'was experimental and precarious'.[48] The twenty-seven men were confirmed by name in their appointments as temporary Justices in a further provisional measure in 1923.[49] Their ability, character and imagination provided the best possible bridge between the system now coming to its end and the properly constituted courts of the new State. Their courts had slipped with as little disruption as possible into the place of the Parish Courts: their title only lent weight to their professional qualification and authority, suggesting a jurisdiction that corresponded to the Dáil District Court as it did in geographical area also. Since these were summary courts, it was easier to begin from scratch, because of the brevity of most proceedings. The justices stressed their nationalist origin, their perception of themselves as servants of the people and their respect for the Dáil judges they replaced.[50]

From the start, proceedings in the District Court were reported in great detail by local newspapers. It may not be a current phenomenon, but it was the most notable feature of the provincial press for many years. Moreover, it was often the same justice whose decisions and pronouncements were being reported over the same period in the same newspaper. Of the twenty-seven justices appointed as a stop-gap in November 1922 to replace the forty-two Resident Magistrates and innumerable Justices of the Peace, by 1960 some of them were still presiding in the same districts to which they had been first appointed.[51] Sir James O'Connor, author of the standard work on summary jurisdiction, *The Irish Justice of the Peace*, wrote the preface for Gavan Duffy's new edition of the book in 1925 and graciously condescended to give advice to neophyte justices, most of it breathtakingly superficial. He also indulged in a forecast that deserves an honoured place in any list of failed prophecies: 'With the arrival of dapper and efficient District Justices, something of the joy that comes from the highly dramatic instinct of the Irish people will be gone.'[52] The company of his peers of the Bar and Bench had insulated the writer in easy assumptions which could have been quickly shed by the perusal of any country newspaper.

Even while the plans for a new judicial framework were clamouring for attention, another legacy of the revolutionary jurisdiction was signalling frantically for official notice. It succeeded in capturing an extraordinary share of time and paperwork, engaged the Ministries of Home Affairs and Finance in another bout of *étatisme* and overflowed into the domains of the Attorney General, the Revenue Commissioners and the Accountant General of His Majesty's Customs and Excise. Shortly after the appointment of Crowley as a Judicial Commissioner, Sheehan, Assistant Secretary at Home Affairs, raised the question of the arrears of salary due to him and to Professor Clery as Dáil judges, salaries that had not been paid but which had been accumulated on O'Friel's advice. In the memorandum, he noted that both men had been considered disloyal, but, in Crowley's case, on 'the arguable issue' that he had conducted himself correctly and that it was wrong of the government to suppress the Dáil Courts.[53] The Ministry knew that Meredith and Davitt continued to be paid their salaries because they came out of its own estimate. In his reply, the masterly Cornelius Gregg moved the goalposts. Eschewing the abstract question of judicial office, he instead pointed out, reasonably enough that Meredith and Davitt had continued to work for the State and Crowley had not. Unfortunately, sure of his ground on that issue, he yielded hostages to fortune by generously adding that 'in equity' there might be some claim arising from the sudden termination of office, but the question would have to abide the reorganisation of the judiciary.[54] Such a statement lent credence to the view that the inherent jurisdiction of the Republican Supreme Court had not been brought to an end by the establishment of another judiciary. While Crowley had certainly made some application for salary not paid to him – possibly as a result of a conversation with Meredith, who revealed that he and Davitt continued to be paid – the impetus to move the question to ministerial level came from O'Friel in order to face down Gregg on the specific issue and to win some posthumous recognition for the validity of the Dáil Courts. It was he who drafted the statement for his Minister to present to the Executive Council on 4 February 1924,[55] which subtly highlighted the impropriety of the government continuing to pay salaries to judges whom it deemed loyal, while ignoring the claims of two others because of their personal convictions.

It was understood that Professor Clery would in no way seek or accept a pension from a government he despised, but in the penultimate paragraph of the memorandum the question was raised of whether the Dáil Courts had been finally abolished or if they would be when the Courts of Justice Bill (then being debated in the Seanad) was enacted and whether, on abolition, compensation should be paid to its judges 'whose tenure is stated to have been for life'.[56] Although the Executive Council agreed to the payment of arrears to Crowley, the Ministry of Finance had still not moved on the issue by the time the Free State Courts of Justice were inaugurated and Meredith was made a Judge of the High Court. When he was not promoted to Chief Judicial Commissioner in succession, Crowley resigned. He was now free to concentrate on the question of salary since August 1922 and to pursue a claim to be paid £750 for life as a judge duly appointed by Dáil Éireann. John O'Byrne, then Attorney General, to whom the problem was referred, was unambiguous in his advice:

> Followed as it [the Decree of 29 June 1920 authorising the establishment of courts] was by the act of the Minister for Home Affairs in setting up Courts and appointing Judges, and having regard to the fact that these Courts continued for a considerable time to function with the approval and under the authority of Dáil Eireann, it must, in my opinion, be assumed that the Courts, as set up, were set up in pursuance of the said Decree and that the said constitution was *intra vires*.[57]

This positive statement contrasts sharply with the equally positive statement made two years before by his predecessor, Hugh Kennedy: 'As you are aware, the Ministry is of the opinion that the late Minister's decree purporting to establish Courts was wholly illegal and not authorised by Dáil Decrees'.[58] There had already been considerable delay in paying the arrears and then only after the Ministry of Finance had recouped the pension that Crowley received as a former British official, but paid by the Irish side under post-Treaty agreements. The Accountant and Comptroller-General of the Custom House in London was demanding the repayment of an amount of £41.14s on observing that its pensioner had been working as a Judicial Commissioner from 17 August 1923 to 31

January following; he thus filled an office in a public department under Section 20 of the Superannuation Act of 1834. The Order in Council of March 1922 specifically extended that section to include office in the Irish Free State, so that those civil servants who were content to serve new masters would not be in the fortunate position of having a job and a pension for a corresponding job at the same time. Crowley, ever the disputant, queried the definition of 'public department' and lodged a counter-claim with the Custom House for the portion of the pension withheld while he was a British prisoner,[59] and which had been restored from April 1922, solely through the representations made on his behalf by the Irish Ministry of Finance. He felt no difference on that score in his castigations of the same department for putting obstacles in his path to full remuneration. Nor did he allude – strangely, no one did – to the fact that he had received full remuneration from Dáil funds in respect of the period of detention.

Memoranda, correspondence and inter-departmental minutes continued to augment the files in the Government Secretariat, the Departments of Justice and of Finance – as their titles evolved during the *longueurs* of the issue – as well as the London interest and the Revenue Commissioners. The single-mindedness of the man remains a puzzle: the motive does not appear to be need or greed. Crowley regularly spent time in Paris at good addresses and travelled to America on at least two occasions – ostensibly to follow the Republican funds there in the pursuit of his determination to be paid £750, free of income tax, for the rest of his life. It would be an exaggeration to say that O'Friel encouraged him, but in his subtle way the Secretary drew attention to the claim in words that suggested a particular response and in a direction that reinforced the possibility that it would be taken seriously. In the absence of private correspondence or reminiscences, one can only surmise from the great weight of documents in official files, but in this, as in his direction of the Winding-up Commission, it is difficult not to discern a skilful guiding of the establishment to acknowledge not only the legitimacy, but the primacy, of the Dáil Courts. There is also evident a certain determination to get the better of the rather grand Gregg on each and every issue. Departmental rivalry aside, it was Gregg and his colleagues who held the purse strings and O'Friel who had to manoeuvre his way around the obstacles.

Spurred by the Attorney General's advice and Crowley's unremitting rearguard attacks, a Bill to provide the former judges with a pension of £500 was put in hand and was passed in 1925.[60] The only person who benefited was Crowley. In the cases of Meredith and Davitt, the pension was suspended while they held public office and Clery made only a bare acknowledgment of the letter from the Minister inviting him to apply for a pension. However, the State was to discover that it would not get rid of Mr Crowley's pretensions as easily as that. As soon as Fianna Fáil became the party of government in 1932, he renewed his claim for the full sum of £750, and the various department files were unearthed and began to increase once more. Stephen Roche, Assistant Secretary, urged his Minister to be cautious: 'I know Mr Crowley well & am familiar with all the facts of his case ... [and] recommend that no notice be taken of his present letter.'[61] The applicant succeeded in making personal representations to the Attorney General, to the Minister for Finance, and to the Minister for Justice. He then issued High Court proceedings against the last two on 8 February 1934, in which he sought a declaration that he had been appointed a Judge of the Supreme Court of the Irish Republic for life and was entitled to a salary of £750 from 15 August 1920 until his death. Although he asked for an account to be taken, nowhere in his pleadings did Crowley aver to the pension of which he had been in receipt since 1925.[62] The Attorney General at the time was Conor Maguire and he had, of course, served with the plaintiff as a judge under Dáil Éireann. Patrick Ruttledge, the Minister for Justice, and one of the two defendants, was de Valera's deputy, whose approval Crowley had solicited before he accepted the appointment to the Winding-up Commission in August 1923. If further irony were needed, the subpoenas to the witnesses were issued in the name of the Chief Justice, as was customary – none other than Hugh Kennedy, who had anathematised the Dáil Courts as illegal and counselled their discontinuance. Having seen them safely subsumed into the jurisdiction of the High Court almost a decade previously, it must have begun to seem as if he would never be rid of them. Crowley's close association with these varied personalities during the heady days of revolution was to be of little advantage now that they occupied posts of grave responsibility in the State. It was the measure of his *naïveté* that he failed to grasp that reality.

The case was heard by Mr Justice Johnston, who had been County Court Judge in Monaghan and a member of the Judiciary Committee.

He delivered judgement on 30 July 1934. While it is a fair-minded exposition of the facts and an examination of the applicable law, it fairly crackles with disapproval at times. As a former judge under the British administration, Johnston must have been acutely aware that had he been forced into retirement in 1924, instead of being fortunate enough to have been *persona grata* to the new State and thus elevated to high judicial office, he would not have been entitled to a pension equivalent to that which Crowley had been getting for an unconscionably short service. The judgement stressed that the plaintiff had accepted a pension for the past seven years without question, in place of salary for an office that had been terminated by the State; he could not therefore deny that he had acquiesced and he could not say now that he had no title to that money. 'Mr Crowley has been treated not only justly but even generously by his country and I think this claim of his is ungracious.' The judge referred to Crowley's retirement in early middle age from the Customs service to live on his savings and a small pension. Having been called to the Bar, he had unexpectedly been given an office for which he got a pension of £500 per annum, in spite of having served for only a bare two years, but he still was not satisfied. 'Most of the young men who, risking everything, went out into the wilderness in 1919 would, I feel sure, have been content to say "and wilderness were Paradise enow",' he said as he dismissed the claims with costs.[63] The scorn did little to silence Crowley: he sent off a further series of reprimands to de Valera and Seán T. O'Kelly and then wrote a pamphlet on how the members of Fianna Fáil had disgraced their republican principles in their treatment of him; he called it 'Step by Step. From the Republic Back into Empire' subtitled 'The Evolution of Eamonn [*sic*] de Valera.'[64] He continued to be paid his pension and died in 1954.

Mr Justice Johnston may have believed that the young men of 1919 were content to remain in the wilderness of non-recognition twenty years on, even if they saw all around them others who, in the common mantra of post-independence Ireland, 'had played their part in the national struggle' being given some reward, however modest. None of them was in a position to mount the kind of high-powered bid that Diarmuid Crowley was able to. Many who had sacrificed as much as he had, and more, were fortunate enough to secure positions in the new court service, although only a fraction of those who applied could be accommodated in

1922 and later.[65] There were others who had taken up arms against the Free State or who had remained aloof from its administration, because of their strong Republican convictions. Some of them thought, as Crowley had done, that with the advent of Fianna Fáil right would triumph. Mrs Heron and Mrs Ceannt, judges of the District Court for Pembroke and Rathmines, felt that they might now safely forward the balance of monies kept in the National Land Bank since October 1922; on 18 January 1934 they sent a cheque for £19.18s.3d to the Minister for Finance and closed the account.[66] After the Government extended the IRA pension to those who had fought in the Civil War, some former Dáil Court personnel who had refused to cooperate with the Free State felt that their service should also be recognised. The Dáil Courts (1919–22) Association was formed around 1935 and made representations to Eamon de Valera as President of the Executive Council.[67] It was claimed, correctly, that members had often stood in as much danger as the fighting men and should be equally eligible for pensions. They should get preference in appointments to the court service and where former Dáil judges and clerks had died, financial help with their children's education should be given.

But among the purists, there was disapproval of even this belated action. Sinn Féin, at its committee meeting on 30 November 1935, gave permission for an office to be used for a meeting of the Dáil Éireann Court officials who opposed any claims being made in respect of compensation 'for services rendered to the Government and Parliament of the Republic'.[68] They need not have troubled themselves; no official recognition, then or later, was accorded to the men and women who took part, at considerable sacrifice and risk, in this foolhardy enterprise whose legacy endured in the particular structure of the jurisdiction established in 1924 and which remains unchanged in its essentials today. A public tribute came, fittingly enough, from one of the District Justices appointed in October 1922. William Coyne wrote a simple book called *The Law Courts in Eire* to celebrate twenty-one years of Irish administration of the law. The dedication reads:

This book is dedicated to all those Parish and District Judges, both priests and laymen, who manned the Republican Courts under the authority of Dáil Eireann during the critical years Nineteen-Nineteen, Nineteen-Twenty, Nineteen-Twenty-one. It is to their splendid example of heroism and patriotic services, rendered without hope of reward at a crucial period in our country's history, is largely due the ultimate transfer of the legal system from English to Irish hands.[69]

It is arguable whether such a large claim could reasonably be made for the Dáil Court system, but the 'ultimate transfer' referred to by Justice Coyne was marked by a certain measure of triumphalism on 11 June 1924. Two years before, Sir James Molony, Lord Chief Justice, had reluctantly agreed, on Kennedy's urging, to allow the words 'Rialtas Sealadach na hÉireann' to be superimposed at the head of future High Court proceedings. In his letter of 15 July 1922,[70] he added that he expected that there would be a considerable influx of business into these courts now that the Republican Courts had been brought to an end, although the decree to that effect was not made until ten days later. Kennedy may or may not have been aware that around the same time Molony had gone over to London, accompanied by Sir John Ross, the Irish Lord Chancellor, to confer with highly placed officials on the future of the judges in the new order.[71] Although the representatives of the Irish judiciary expressed anxiety on the ability of the Provisional Government to impose law and order, they were even more worried about their pensions and probable loss of office. It seemed at first that the British government might be persuaded to indemnify their entitlements under the Treaty arrangements regarding pensions to those who held office during the transition, but initial sympathy gave way as the demands increased, and the advice ultimately conveyed was that the judges should work out their problems with the Provisional Government without intervention from London.[72] Having no other prospects, the British-appointed judges continued to preside at their unchanged courts until released by the jurisdiction of the constitutional courts, which came into existence in 1924.[73] Hugh Kennedy was appointed to be the first Chief Justice: there were two other Supreme Court Judges and six members of the High Court. The Governor General, Tim Healy, administered the oath of office to him to June 1924, and the following day he, as Chief Justice, administered the oath to his eight brethren:

I do solemnly and sincerely before God promise and declare that I will duly and faithfully execute the office of [judge] of Saorstát Éireann without fear or favour, affection or ill will towards any man and that I will uphold the constitution of Saorstát Éireann by law established.

The first pledge by a judge on Irish soil to serve the law of the people, and not the sovereign's, was made in a formal ceremony at Dublin Castle. The *Freeman's Journal*, surprisingly, complained that the event 'was shorn of all the pomp and circumstance of the old days'.[74] Even more surprisingly, the *Irish Times* was impressed with the 'elaborate and impressive ceremony. Troops drawn up in the Upper Castle Yard to give military *éclat* to the occasion … and with the Dublin Metropolitan Police formed a guard of honour that would do credit to any state ceremony anywhere'.[75] The only judges of bygone days present were those who were there as participants and none came for the comradely gesture of passing on the judicial torch. Mr Justice Charles O'Connor had been Master of the Rolls: Mr Justice William Johnston, a County Court judge far-sighted enough to have offered his services while the ink was still drying on the Treaty, had been suitably rewarded.[76] One of the most intriguing survivors in the Upper Yard on 11 June 1924 must surely have been Mr Justice William Evelyn Wylie who had, as a British officer, prosecuted William Cosgrave at the court martial following the 1916 Rebellion.[77] Both men would have had good reason to be grateful in the unseasonal June drizzle that Wylie had recommended the reprieve of the death sentence passed on Lieutenant Cosgrave at the time. Also prominent among the dignitaries present was James Campbell, the Attorney General who had refused Wylie's request that the captured men should be allowed defence counsel.[78] In the intervening eight years he had acquired a different name and office and was now Lord Glenavy, Chairman of Seanad Éireann. The *Freeman's Journal* shook a final fist at the newly *ancien régime*:

From the chambers of the old Privy Council where the 'practices' of the old external tyranny were devised and directed Ireland's own judges proceeded to the new Supreme Court where the oath of loyalty to the Free State and to the ideal of impartial justice was taken by the future administrators of Irish law. … No department of the old order in Ireland was more poisoned in its effects upon Irish social life than the Department of Justice. In every conflict where the civic rights of the common people conflicted with the interests of the dominant class, the scales were heavily weighted against the people.[79]

British judges being reborn into an Irish establishment was not the only translation happening in the Upper Castle Yard. James Creed Meredith, the Chief Judicial Commissioner of the Dáil Courts, left his court in the imposing building to the right of the gate and stepped out to become Mr Justice Meredith of the High Court. He sat on Commission business and Mr Commissioner Crowley paid tribute to his work and would miss him. They had been associated in dangerous times and had enjoyed the best of good feeling and friendship, which could also be said of those who had served in Republican courts as well as Meredith's colleagues in the Commission. The latter quoted Macaulay: 'The Romans were like brothers in the brave days of old.' It was again the surprising *Irish Times* which made the connection in its report the following day, under the heading, 'Dáil Éireann Courts – Mr Justice Meredith'.[80] In the conscious effort which was made to achieve balance in the newly created Bench, Meredith – economically, one might say – filled two different criteria: he was from a Protestant unionist background and he was an Irish nationalist. There could be no confusion about Mr Justice Fitzgibbon of the Supreme Court: he had recently been TD for Trinity College, Dublin. When Charles O'Connor was Master of the Rolls, he had enraged the British government and earned the grateful remembrance of nationalists because he had ordered the arrest on attachment warrant of General Macready, commander of Crown forces in Ireland, and of other high-ranking personages in July 1921: they had failed to produce two prisoners who had applied for orders of habeas corpus. The case was a mirror image of that of George Plunkett except that the British, although made exceedingly cross by the whole incident, forebore to throw *their* judge in jail. Like Wylie, he was preferred for judicial office by the Irish government. He and Mr Justice Murnaghan from Northern Ireland were Roman Catholics. Two other new judges had served in the lower courts, Thomas Shaughnessy, the popular Recorder for Dublin, and County Court Judge Johnston. It was, without any attempt at a pun, a most judicious mix.

Since Hugh Kennedy was a great preserver of correspondence, it may be assumed that the only recently discarded judge who wrote to him was Mr Justice Dodd because his letter is with the Kennedy papers.[81] He wrote the next day gracefully, pledging his loyalty to the Chief Justice as the head of 'our profession'. He added, somewhat enigmatically, 'You have a great opportunity, one denied to the old judges for various reasons'. In spite of the vague implication, Dodd did not return to practice at the Irish Bar, nor did any of his colleagues. Sir James O'Connor, who as Lord Justice O'Connor had addressed a lengthy memorandum to the Judiciary Committee on how matters should be disposed in the new order, applied before the end of the decade to be readmitted as a solicitor: the application came before Chief Justice Kennedy in 1929.[82] By that time, the rebuilding of the Four Courts was nearly finished. The Chief Justice looked forward to making an occasion of the move from Dublin Castle but his excitement was effectively doused by the Minister for Justice, James Fitzgerald-Kenney. No money could be spared for unnecessary display in difficult financial times, and, even more importantly, there was the security aspect. Those who had burned Gandon's masterpiece of a building, or their successors, were out there waiting to do it again. Drawing attention to the move would only provide the incentive. 'No advantage can be derived from shaking a red flag in the face of an insane bull'.[83] The Order was made transferring the several Courts of Justice from Dublin Castle to King's Inn Quay from 1 October 1931. Kennedy would not willingly forego some celebration of the event. He suggested, *sub rosa*, that religious services be held by different denominations to mark the opening of the Law Term and, having attended Mass at the parish of St Michan's in the vicinity of the Four Courts, he proceeded to the Supreme Court. Sir Philip Hanson of the Office of Public Works was present to receive the Chief Justice's congratulations on the work of restoration:

> I am proud to take my place here in a building which represents so much of Irish art, Irish craftsmanship and Irish labour. I would ask you, Sir Philip, to convey this expression of appreciation to your Board and officials.[84]

The name of the Board's architect, Mr Byrne, would be forever linked with that of Gandon. Whatever about the soldiers of the rearguard, Hugh Kennedy ensured there were enough events to catch the notice of the national press for the next day.

The legal way of life resumed at the Four Courts and continued unaltered, except in the persons of the judges, just as it had in the Dáil Courts. As Ronan Fanning has written, 'Irish law remained wedded to British traditions. Cases were heard in the same courtrooms, often conducted by the same lawyers in the same antique garb of wig and gown. As late as 1932, after the change of Government, only one of the three Supreme Court judges and none of the seven high court judges did not bear the initials KC (King's Counsel) after his name. And the Irish inns of court are to this day the King's Inns.'[85]

Over the years, most of the men prominent in the legal administration of the First Dáil, or in its immediate aftermath, achieved public office or civil service appointments. Gavan Duffy, who had resigned from government because of the suppression of the Dáil Courts, became President of the High Court. He was succeeded in that office by Conor Maguire, who later became Chief Justice. Cahir Davitt was then made President of the High Court. Both Dan Browne and Kevin O'Shiel were Judicial Land Commissioners. All the members of the Dáil Courts Winding-up Commission became judges of one kind or another – James Creed Meredith being elevated to the Supreme Court in 1940 – with the exception of Diarmuid Crowley. George Nicholls and Philip McQuaid were County Registrars of Galway and Clare respectively. T.V. Cleary, who had been dismissed from his position of Registrar to the Dáil Supreme Court in August 1922, later served as the Chief Clerk of the District Court. The other members of the Home Affairs team, Crump, McKeon and O'Toole, were transferred to the High Court in 1924. Of the women workers, Madge Clifford, Kathleen Bulfin and Kay Barry had left the Ministry by the end of May 1922. Nora Brick was suspended and then dismissed when she confessed to having helped the Republican side as a Red Cross nurse in July 1922: the quality of mercy was to be strained in one direction only.[86] Mrs Heron who, with Mrs Ceannt, had forwarded to Seán McEntee the credit balance in the Rathmines Court account, also made representations to him on behalf of Marian Duggan, a barrister and a former Dáil Court official, urging that she be made a District Justice.[87] However, it was not until 1963 that Eileen Kennedy was appointed the first woman judge of the constitutional courts; her courtroom was crowded for days with people coming to witness the novelty of it all. She also thereby broke another precedent; she was the first female to sit in a court with her head uncovered.[88]

The court in which she sat was that of the Republic of Ireland and had been for the previous decade and more. An observer, who had attended a Parish Court in Lixnaw or Lacken forty odd years before, would have remarked on the familiarity of subject matter and procedure, although conducted in the grandeur of the Four Courts. He might have ruefully reflected that the peasants had captured the castle but had sensibly decided not to alter the interior. That might have struck him as odd given the exaltation, the danger and the trauma that had accompanied the first steps of the journey to where he now stood. It was the growing strength of the movement for independence that encouraged individuals or groups to initiate experiments in self-sufficiency and communities to accept and support them. This was true both of the tribunals which tried to neutralise the intimidating violence long associated with land hunger and of the assumption of the role of village constabulary by the Volunteers. They could have succeeded only to the extent of the support of the law-abiding majority. Once the normal structure of law and order was diminished by the deepening political struggle and it became a matter of national pride to demonstrate a commitment to the symbols of separatism, it was clear that hearts and minds had been won for whatever legal organisation Dáil Éireann could construct on that foundation. For it must be stressed that, apart from west Clare where a system was in place, legal self-help was spontaneous and localised, even though it was manifest throughout the country by mid-1920. Almost a year separated the two decrees governing courts passed by the Dáil, it was the outline scheme for the arbitration courts which was chiefly in operation up to the Truce, although criminal trials were taking place. Austin Stack was not in a position to impose the central administration of the Dáil Courts proper until August 1921.

With hazard and hardship behind them, the courts entered a long period of activity, disciplined by administration and the inbuilt hierarchy of judicial authority. A political theorist – or a British judge – would understandably have found their status questionable, but in a short time they had become the established courts by public usage, if not by immutable law. Procedure, law and precedent were those of the courts they replaced: the difference was in external matters – surroundings, dress, the absence of sonorous titles, although that aspect changed somewhat after the Treaty. Apart from the act of defiance constituted by their very existence, there was nothing of a revolutionary court in the way business was conducted or in the run of decisions. In harmony with most legal systems of the time and of long after, they were primarily concerned with the protection of property rather than the well-being of persons. No order, social or procedural, was overturned, and that may explain their rapid integration. Cicero said that in war the laws are silent, but, at their best, the local courts represented the determination that civil decencies would prevail. At the height of their powers, they were struck down and from the least expected quarter. And, more bewildering was the detraction heaped upon the courts at the moment of their demise by those who had established them and without whose support they could not have existed. They were cut off with little thought of their replacement or of relief for the frustration of thousands of litigants. Within another year, in an extraordinary piece of juridical *déjà vu*, a lengthy and expensive commission revived, not only those cases cut off in their prime, but any other matter that a participant might wish to be rejudicated. After a comparatively short time, all these decided cases were absorbed by the new High Court of the newly independent Ireland, and in time most of those involved in the higher ranks of the Dáil Courts and their administration were remembered in terms of appointments to office. The majority of the workers, who were not so fortunate, had their memories and an experience denied to those who had remained aloof. On the other hand, there were those who had died because the impudence of the courts upset authority and there were those who were too old or too humble to appreciate what they had achieved. Perhaps the most elegiac figure is Austin Stack, whom a kinder Fate would surely have allowed the small triumph of being a barrister and citing a Dáil Court precedent to a bewigged judge of the Irish Free State. He might have been surprised to see the wealth of files gathering dust over the years in the Public Record Office, disturbed only by academics or the occasional civil servant to confirm a reference, and hardly ever by the curious laity.

In the final analysis, of course, the people had set up these courts for themselves, not for posterity, even if they were making their own history. Political violence and the reaction to it ensured the disruption of the norms of law and order which coincided with the imposition by Dáil Éireann of a uniform judicial administration; but, before that happened, the local policing of districts by the Volunteers and the praiseworthy efforts to settle land disputes without bloodshed were already matters of widespread, but separate, practice. Popular courts, with judges elected from and by the community, were sufficiently well rooted to survive underground during the worst of the Black-and-Tan war: they were already well in position to profit fully from the peace which the Truce brought. The fact of their survival was due to local officials, and not at all to the central authority of the Dáil, which could be effective only when communication was possible once again. A year later, when the courts were struck down from within, it became politically correct to castigate them for assuming a jurisdiction they had not been given, but no one asked why should they not have done so. Licensing matters were traditionally dealt with by local courts and these were the only local courts then functioning. Nor should it have been reprehensible to force an opponent to prosecute his claim in the only jurisdiction one had been commanded to recognise. If these were faults, they were ignored until it suited the government to become exercised on the issue. The expediency with which it closed down the courts was ill-judged, and the same government was forced to reinstate them in a more expensive and elaborate guise. However, it was entirely due to the vigilance and perseverance of politicians that the principle of judicial independence was copperfastened in the courts which finally emerged in 1924.

Notes

Chapter 1

1   *United Irishman*, 9 December 1905.

2   R.F. Foster, *Modern Ireland 1600–1972* (London, 1988), p. 432. On the metamorphosis of Sinn Féin over a period of years, Foster writes: 'The importance of Sinn Fein was that it continued providing a haven for various fringe movements, publishing yet another declamatory newspaper, advocating its vague and purist nostrums for theoretical "independence", and it would be there after 1916 establishing an ostensible continuity between turn-of-the-century cultural revivalism and the new revolution. But by then, it would be a different organization, operating on different terms,' p. 458.

3   Richard Davis, *Arthur Griffith and Non-violent Sinn Féin* (Dublin, 1974), pp. 23–4.

4   National Library of Ireland, The Constitution of Sinn Féin.

5   The argument for and against abstention from Westminster had waxed and waned since O'Connell's time. Davis, op.cit., chapter 3.

6   Brian Farrell, *The Founding of Dáil Eireann* (Dublin, 1971).

7   The staid reporting of early newspapers was ambivalent about the obvious preparation for political violence-drilling and possession of guns – but endorsed the swift punishment of petty crime. Remarks by some District Justices in the 1950s suggest that this romanticised view of persons convicted for possession of weapons was still fashionable.

8   *Limerick Leader*, 4 February 1920.

9   The Defence of the Realm Act 1914 was introduced as a war measure to protect national security; its draconian powers were greatly extended by the Restoration of Order in Ireland Act 1920. Charles Townshend, *Political Violence in Ireland* (Oxford, 1983), chapters 6 and 7.

10   *Limerick Leader*, 8 March 1920.

11   The Wyndham Act 1903 was a coherent scheme for tenant-purchase which was voluntary. Dáil Éireann established a Land Commission and a Land Court, which enshrined the principle of compulsory purchase.

12   *Limerick Leader*, 13 August 1919.

13   *Limerick Leader*, 11 June 1920.

14   *Freeman's Journal*, 4 June 1920.

15   *Tipperary People,* 4 June 1920.

16   *Tipperary People,* 18 June 1920.

17 Boards of Guardians insisted that doctors make declarations for the committal of a person to an asylum before a Republican justice.
18 Reported in *Limerick Leader*, 21 July 1920.
19 Leon O'Broin, *W. E. Wylie and the Irish Revolution 1916–1921* (Dublin, 1989), p. 86.
20 No plaintiffs or defendants had appeared because all the cases had been settled at the local Sinn Féin Court the previous Saturday. *Limerick Leader*, 16 June 1920.
21 J.P. Casey, 'The Genesis of the Dáil Courts' (1973) 9 *Irish Jurist* (n.s.) 326.
22 Outline of the Constitution of the West Clare Courts, 3. J. Anthony Gaughan, *Austin Stack, Portrait of a Separatist* (Tralee, 1977), Appendix 5 Dublin.
23 Ibid., p. 102.
24 *The Constructive Work of Dáil Eireann*, No. 1, compiled and edited by Erskine Childers, Dublin, 1921, pp. 13–14. The framework was already reaching beyond mere arbitration: why else give a right to appeal and a hierarchical structure if parties had agreed in advance to accept the arbitrators' decision?
25 'Memories of My Lifetime', a series of twelve articles by Kevin O'Shiel published in the *Irish Times,* November 1966.
26 Tony Varley, 'Agrarian Crime as Social Control; Sinn Fein and the Land Question in the West of Ireland in 1920' in *Whose Law and Order? Aspects of Crime* and *Social Control in Irish Society*, eds. Mike Tomilson, Tony Varley and Ciaran McCullagh, Sociological Association of Ireland, Belfast, 1988, pp. 54–7.
27 O'Sheil, op.cit.
28 Conor Maguire, 'The Republican Court', *Capuchin Annual*, 1968.
29 Kevin O'Shiel was quoted as stressing that it was not a district court but a High Commission appointed directly by the Substitute Minister for Agriculture for the Republican Government to inquire into and adjudicate on all land disputes, and by his warrant he had a firm and absolute voice in all his adjudication, *Limerick Leader*, 23 June 1920.
30 Tom Maguire was the officer in command of the local Volunteers. He was sympathetic to the claimants and was initially reluctant to assist in the enforcement of the decision, Varley, op. cit., p. 62.
31 The IRA was never at ease with the time and energy expended on servicing the duplication of a civil administration, but on the other hand they tried to dominate when there was a clash of wills. See David Fitzpatrick, *Politics and Irish Life 1913–1921* (Dublin 1977), pp. 179–80.
32 Dorothy Macardle, *The Irish Republic,* Corgi edition (London, 1968), p. 402.
33 O'Shiel, op.cit.
34 J. Anthony Gaughan, *Austin Stack, Portrait of a Separatist* (Tralee, 1977), pp. 275–6.

Chapter 2

1 J.P. Casey, 'The Genesis of the Dáil Courts' (1974) 9 *Irish Jurist* (n.s.) 326. Professor Casey traces the progress of the Dáil scheme for arbitration courts from June 1919 to their establishment.

2   *The Constructive Work of Dáil Eireann*, No.1, Dublin, 1921, pp. 13–14.

3   James Casey, 'Republican Courts in Ireland 1919–1922' (1970) 5 *Irish Jurist* (n.s.) 325.

4   Dáil Éireann, Minutes of Proceedings 1919–1922, p. 178.

5   UCD Archives, Kennedy Papers P4/1067.

6   Cahir Davitt, 'The Civil Jurisdiction of the Courts of Justice in the Irish Republic 1920–1922', (1968) 3 *Irish Jurist* (n.s.) pp. 121–2.

7   Rules and Forms of Parish and District Court. Department of Home Affairs, 1921 [referred to as 'The Judiciary'] NA, PROI, DE u/J79. DE 11/179 also D/Jus H 140/ 5.

8   Chapter 6, infra.

9   Bunreacht na h-Eireann 1937 Article 35.4.1.

10   Some of the committee may have protested: in the copy later presented by Mr Justice Maguire to the National Library of Ireland, the passage is underlined.

11   Under the British system, some crimes were tried by the County Court judge at Quarter Sessions, more serious offences were tried at the Assizes held three times a year in each county, at which judges of the King's Bench and, sometimes, the Lord Chief Justice, presided. Under the Dáil system, the Circuit Judge sitting alone dealt with serious crime, but from about March 1922 juries were again summoned.

12   Davitt had generous praise for the calibre of the District Judges who sat with him and said that he rarely disagreed with them on the facts of a case. Davitt, p. 62.

13   Maguire, op.cit.

14   Seán Ó hUadhaigh, a well-known solicitor, was on the Standing Committee of Sinn Féin up to 1930. His advice was sought on many topics during the period of the first Dáil, and he kept the Dáil Courts up to scratch by complaining frequently and pugnaciously about delays on behalf of his numerous clients (see NA, DE 13/ 4 under 'O'). As a member of the Urban District Council for Kingstown, he was instrumental in having its name changed to Dun Laoghaire.

15   Arthur Griffith's address to the National Convention, reported in *United Irishman*, 9 December 1905.

16   *Freeman's Journal*, 4 June 1920.

17   *Law Society Gazette*, Vol. XIV, No. 5 November 1920, which referred to the reply on Arbitration Courts given in June 1920.

18   (1920) 54 *Irish Law Times*, 26 June 1920 and 273, 6 November 1920.

19   Davitt's recollections are mirrored in newspaper reports from mid-1920.

20   W.H. Brayden, 'Republican Courts in Ireland', *Journal of the American Bar Association*, September 1920, printed as a pamphlet by the Benjamin Franklin Bureau, Chicago.

21   'It must not be forgotten that a submission to arbitration is essentially a contract, viz., a mere agreement between parties to submit to an arbitrator or arbitrators. It is therefore an inappropriate form or procedure where any pressure is brought to bear on any party', NA, DE 10/6, Meredith to Stack, 12 October 1921.

22   Assizes judges in Limerick were forced to accept the hospitality of Lord Dunraven at Adare Manor because their usual lodgings were refused to them and courts were held behind barricades with a military guard. *Limerick Leader*, 15 July 1920.

23 Infra, Chapter 3.

24 *Tipperary People*, 8 July 1920. The parties were asked to submit to the jurisdiction of the court, but were referred to as plaintiffs and defendants. One of the decisions, in which a claimant whose mother had given up possession of a farm thirty-three years previously and who was preferred over a contract purchaser, appears to have been in breach of the Dáil decree no. 6 which was passed on 29 June 1920 under which such claims could be pursued only by special leave.

25 *Limerick Leader*, 16 July 1920. Alderman Stephen O'Mara, a famous Limerick man, refused to give his name and was released only after he had been identified.

Chapter 3

1 NA, DE 9/1-3, DE 11/8, DE 25/1, 4. After the Provisional Government was set up, Eamonn Duggan, Minister for Home Affairs, was worried about issuing passports when he wrote to Kennedy that it went against Dáil policy on emigration. UCD Archives, Kennedy Papers, P 4/10.

2 NA, DE 11/94. Home Affairs would set an enquiry on foot when a complaint was made of a breach either by a company or an individual. Businesses and individuals were boycotted in return, often only on the basis of rumour, apparently.

3 The wealth of records of the Dáil Éireann Courts, formerly in the Public Records Office, now part of the National Archives, bears this out.

4 Gaughan, op. cit., pp. 102–49.

5 In fairness, it must be noted that his letters to de Valera are businesslike and confident (NA, DE 11/90), those few to women, gentle and chivalrous (DE 11/40) – and on 8 October 1921 he wrote a warm letter to Davitt, who had apologised for mistaking the date of court fixtures: 'I could not bring myself to find fault with you even if you made a big slip considering how you have gone along for the past twelve months or so without putting a foot wrong.' NA, DE 10/ 5. Stack to Davitt, 8 October 1921. His letters to his wife (in NLI) are very revealing.

6 Conversations with his sons, Aidan Browne, SC, and the late Donal Browne, State Solicitor for Kerry; also with his friend, Maurice Moynihan, Secretary to the Government 1937–64.

7 NA, D/Jus H 140/1.

8 Madge Clifford corresponded at length with Ernie O'Malley; see O'Malley Papers, UCD Archives.

9 They appear from the lengthy and detailed reports to the Ministry as being men who were capable and shrewd: they worked long hours and moved indefatigably around their areas. NA, DE/11 contains several bulky files on their activities.

10 Arthur Griffith asked for the cooperation of Sinn Féin in having the Dáil decree on Arbitration Courts brought to the attention of the clubs, Committee Minute, 3 July 1919, N/A, Sinn Féin Funds Case, Book 19.

11 Rules and Forms of the *Courts – The Judiciary*.

12 Correspondence with the registrars is contained in the files of each county, NA, DE 10, and in the Ministry's general files.

13   Money and the failure to account properly for it form the major theme of the correspondence, but no court official could have grown rich from salaries which ranged from moderate to meagre, and many of them were left out of pocket when the courts closed.

14   *New Ross Journal*, 2 July 1920.

15   Remarks of Major Herries-Crosbie, a Resident Magistrate who did not conform to the stereotype. Many reports in the *New Ross Journal* show an intelligent and sympathetic response to the changes all around.

16   The arrest of Terence McSwiney was widely reported. Presumably it was noteworthy since it concerned the first citizen of the country's second city.

17   *New Ross Journal*, 21 September 1920.

18   Ibid., 6 August 1920.

19   Cahir Davitt, 'Civil Jurisdiction of Dáil Courts' (1968) 3 *Irish Jurist*, n.s. 122.

20   Cahir Davitt, *Memoir*, p. 37. His account of Stack's instructions confirms the lack of communication and explains the gap in the Ministry's correspondence for this period.

21   Davitt, *Memoir*, Part XI.

22   NA, DE 11/245. The first letter in Crowley's personal file is a notification from T. V. Cleary, the Registrar, of the Spring Circuit Sittings (T.V. Cleary to Crowley, 15 February 1922). There are no letters for the pre-Treaty period, but he was back at work by November 1921.

23   NA, DE 10 contains correspondence with registrars in all districts.

24   Davitt, *Memoir*, pp. 68–9.

25   NA, DE 16/13 Justices of Currans Parish to M.H.A. January 1922.

26   NA, DE 15 Local court registers. Those showing entries of cases prior to June 1921 include Cork, Donegal, Limerick, Longford and Mayo. Not all the registers are there, because when officials were directed to send in all records, many refused to cooperate because of anti-Treaty sentiments.

27   NA, DE 10/14 Punch to Stack, 8 October 1921.

28   NA, DE 12/466 DE 34/ 23. Chapter 7, infra.

29   NA, DE 10/40. Bridget Kennedy, Registrar for West Limerick, to M.H.A., 9 November 1921.

30   Davitt, Memoir, pp. 61–2.

31   Meredith and Clery took circuit sittings in Dublin. NA, DE 36/1–9.

32   NA, DE 10/8 Collins to Stack, 7 July 1921.

33   NA, DE 10/13; Circuit Court judgements given by Davitt in Mid-Cork are dated 2 June 1921.

34   Davitt, Memoir, p. 61.

35   NA, DE 10/7 Report of Registrar, North Cork, for period 3 July 1920–31 July 1921.

36   NA, DE 6/8 17-1415.

37   The Court of Conscience in South Willliam Street, Dublin, was for the collection of small debts and was under the aegis of Dublin Corporation.

38   The sitting was reported in some newspapers.

39   Davitt, Memoir, pp. 46–7. James Creed Meredith had begun his academic career as a divinity student at Trinity College, Dublin, where he excelled in athletics. He was a Doctor of Philosophy and an authority on Kant. He was called to the Bar in 1902, became interested in the nationalist cause and was involved in the Howth gun-running. He was at the centre of the Dáil Courts venture and at their winding up. He later became a Judge of the Supreme Court of Saorstát Éireann and died in 1942. (Conversation with his daughter, Mrs Moira Gillespie.)

40   Arthur Clery practised as a barrister, as well as being a professor of law at UCD. Todd Andrews paints a memorable picture of this courteous, inattentive man, from whom he learned a great deal (C.S. Andrews, *Man of No Property* [Cork, 1982], pp. 43–5). Judge Gerard Burke of Galway, who acted as registrar to Clery in 1922, has also affectionate memories of him (conversation with the author, February 1993). Davitt clearly loved and admired him.

41   Davitt, Memoir, pp. 48–9. (The writer was told of this incident by the late Billy Noyk, Michael's son, who was also a solicitor.)

42   NA, DE 10/16., Childers, President of District Court, Pembroke and Rathmines, to M.H.A., 5 October 1921.

43   NA, DE 10/68. South Tyrone: as late as 6 December 1921 he wrote to the Registrar that the courts had been functioning there satisfactorily up to some months previously, although this letter is one of the only two in the file.

44   NA, DE 27/1. Instructions sent to District Registrars on 9 August 1921, where unspecified retaliation was promised against those who appeared in enemy courts either as plaintiff or defendant. The easier alternative – and one often taken – was to ignore the proceedings, since an injunction ensured that the dispute would get a hearing.

45   O'Higgins, as Minister for Justice, later denied that there was a prohibition on defending an action in British courts. Dáil Debates, Vol. 4, 24 July 1923, c. 1318.

46   The thrust of Sinn Féin policy was to oust the British administration by providing alternative structures in every way possible.

47   The procedure was explained at great length by Creed Meredith, Chief Judicial Commissioner, in delivering judgement; *Collins and Collins*, 7 November 1923, NA, DE 1/1. Examination of applications for injunctions confirms that they were not granted indiscriminately; NA, DE 34/ 1-109.

48   He returns to the theme constantly in letters to the organisers, NA, DE 11/1, 108, 159, 219.

49   NA, DE 27/1.

50   'Once the Courts are established, Comhairle Ceanntair have no authority over them (apart from helping litigants make contact or to boycott enemy courts), but otherwise Court and Court Officials are completely under the jurisdiction of the Minister for Home Affairs and no other person has authority over them.' Stack to E.O. Boyle, West Donegal, 5 July 1921. NA, DE 10/66.

Chapter 4

1 NA, DE 11/ 144. Four files containing details of 'Country Debts'. Solicitors sent default affidavits and a deposit fee to the Minister, who forwarded them to the Registrar of the district where the debtor resided for proceedings to issue. Not only was it inefficient, but all further queries had to be channelled through the department.

2 PRO, Kew, HO45/20094.

3 NA, DE 10/5, D. Ó Maoldomnaigh, Saggart, to Stack, 12 August 1921.

4 Thomas Jones, *Whitehall Diary,* vol. 3, *Ireland 1918–1925,* ed. K. Middlemas, London, 1971.

5 T.P. Coogan, *Michael Collins,* London, 1990, pp. 244–5; also NA, DE Barton Papers 1093.

6 Typed copy headed 'President's Remarks, Police and Courts' n.d., NA, DE 11/90 and Stack to President, 2 November 1921.

7 NA, DE 11, various correspondence with Registrars and organisers. More than three justices were frequently elected, in spite of the regulations and Stack's continuing rebukes.

8 A long-drawn-out dispute occurred in Abbeyfeale, Co. Limerick, where an election on 3 October 1921 for the third justiceship was between a working man and a member of Meenabela Sinn Féin Club. The ITGWU contended that Meenabela was not properly in Abbeyfeale parish; the other side said the workers' union was not fully affiliated at the time of the election. NA, DE 10/40.

9 The action was taken more in sorrow than in anger, but the necessity to take it was never questioned. The petition had been discovered when a local barracks was taken over; the reason why the farmers desperately needed the extra hour was because the British local commander had failed to grasp that country people did not use Greenwich Mean Time, but 'old time'. Edward Ryan of Cappoquin, Co. Waterford was dismissed in March 1922 after a lengthy enquiry. NA, DE 10/39.

10 NA, DE 10/13. Stack to Registrar, Cork City, 17 August 1921; also NA, DE 10/14. to Registrar, North City of Dublin, same sentiments, same date.

11 The same strict attitude runs though his dealings with almost all registrars: one exception was North Cork, where the Registrar, David Barry, was actually urged to send in details of expenses. 'You are doing good work for me and I do not want to see you at any personal loss.' NA, DE 10/11, Ministry to Barry, 12 September 1921: it may, however, have been a personal letter from Browne.

12 NA, DE 10/67. Letter to MHA, 27 July 1921. The sender's name is torn out but was probably Liam Healy.

13 NA, DE 11/159. Eamon Donnelly, Chief Organiser for Ulster, 3 files.

14 NA, DE 11/70. Adjutant General to Secretary, Department of Defence, 12 October 1921. Seamus Grogan, the clerk in question, had threatened the life of the Divisional Commander when the Company was on parade.

15 Hamilton and Aiken, Solicitors, Londonderry, wrote to the Winding-up Commission on 23 September 1923 to say that they had 28 District Court and 55 Parish Court cases at Carndonogh, Co. Donegal, at the time of closure. NA, DE 40/2.

16   Colonel Gretton was a diehard Conservative and a director of Bass Beer, whose sales had been badly affected by the boycott. *Limerick Week Echo*, 20 October 1921.

17   NA, DE 10/15. Stack to E.J. Duggan, Chief Liaison Officer, 19 September 1921. Duggan succeeded Stack as Minister for Home Affairs in January 1922.

18   NA, DE 25/1.

19   NA, DE 27/1.

20   *The Constructive Work of Dáil Éireann No.1*, Dublin, 1921, pp. 29–30, where details are given of some specific sentences.

21   William Coyne, a solicitor from Mayo, was given six months hard labour on a charge of having documents relating to Dáil Éireann in his possession, *Freeman's Journal*, 3 December 1920. Later he was to be among the first District Justices who were appointed in October 1922. John Lynch, the District Registrar for East Limerick, was killed in Dublin in September 1920 and Thomas Shannon, a Clare Justice, the following April, both by Crown forces.

22   NA, DE 41/ 5. Monahan to Registrar, Winding-up Commission, 25 October 1925.

23   NA, DE 10/8 Breathnach, Registrar, South Cork, to Ministry, 9 October 1921.

24   NA, DE 10/7 Registrar; Report for North Cork District, 3 July 1920–31 July 1921. The Ministry wrote 'perhaps you will be able to get these [the missing payments] cleared up now'. MHA to McAuliffe, Registrar, 15 December 1921.

25   NA, DE 27. General Instructions No. 3. 'On no account should Justices adjourn the Court until force has been used to disperse it. Where the instructions previously issued appear to be contradicted by this circular, the former instructions are now cancelled', 24 November 1921.

26   NA, DE 10/17 Harding to MHA, 4 November 1921.

27   NA, DE 10/17 D.I. Scully to Liaison Office, Gresham Hotel, Dublin, 3 November 1921.

28   *Davitt Memoir*, pp. 68–71.

29   NA, DE 10/2, Register, East Cavan, to MHA, 24 November 1921.

30   *The Constructive Work of Dáil Éireann, No. 1*, Dublin, 1921, p. 30.

31   Clery took the Kerry and Cork Circuits in September and October 1921 NA, DE 11/142 a, and Meredith went to Longford, DE 11/141.

32   *Davitt Memoir*, p. 73.

33   NA, DE 10/ 40 Fitzgerald to Stack, 2 December 1921.

34   Ibid., Stack to Fitzgerald. 5 December 1921.

Chapter 5

1   F.S.L. Lyons, *Ireland Since the Famine* (Fontana edition; London, 1971), p. 440.

2   W.S. Churchill, *The World Crisis: The Aftermath*, London, 1929, p. 308.

3   UCD Archives, Kennedy Papers, P/4 272, Kennedy to Duggan, 18 January 1922.

4   NA, S.1., Proclamation 16 January 1922, published in *Iris Oifigiúil*, No. 5, 14 February 1922.

5   Dorothy Macardle, op. cit, pp. 548–80.

6   Dáil Éireann Official Reports, 14 January 1922.

7   NA, G.1. Minutes of Provisional Government Vol. 1, 17 January 1922.

8   NA, DE 27/1.

9   NA, DE 10/64 Liam Sweeney to MHA, 18 January 1922.

10   NA, DE 11/13 Brigade Officer, Monaghan, to Chief of Police.

11   NA, DE 10/62 Nicholls to J.G. Hassett, 18 January 1922.

12   NA, G.1., Minutes of Provisional Government, Vol. 1, 25 January 1922.

13   Ibid., 17 January 1922.

14   UCD Archives, McGilligan Papers, P35/356/93.

15   The dates were 25, 27, 28, 30, 31 January and 1 February 1922. NA, Minutes of Provisional Government, Vol.1.

16   'It was agreed that Republican Courts should continue to function and arrangements to be made whereby the Prisoners sentenced there might be received in the gaols of the Provisional Government' ibid., 20 January 1922.

17   Ibid., 8 March 1922. A memorandum was to be circulated by Duggan and may possibly be that discussed in the following chapter, but there is no further mention of it in the Minutes.

18   Brian Farrell, 'The Drafting of the Irish Free State Constitution: IV' (1971) 6 Part 2 *Irish Jurist* (n.s.) 346.

19   *Davitt Memoir*, pp. 95–6.

20   Griffith said that every government minister was a minister of Dáil Éireann. When Seán T. O'Kelly asked, 'And responsible to Dáil Eireann?', Collins interrupted sharply, 'Certainly not'. Dáil Éireann Official Report, 16 August 1921–8 June 1922, p. 100.

21   UCD Archives, Kennedy Papers, P4/301 (3), (9).

22   NA, DE 11/142. Notification to Judge Clery that the appointment of Gearoid de Burca as Registrar to his Circuit Court had been approved, 18 February 1922.

23   *The Kerry People*, 28 January 1922.

24   *Clare Champion*, 11 February 1922.

25   *Davitt Memoir*, p. 81.

26   Reported in *King's County Chronicle*, 16 March 1922.

27   NA, DE 25/2.

28   NA, D/Jus H 140/1 Nicholls to Secretary, Ministry for Home Affairs, Upper Merrion Street. He suspected that various members were watching to see if he 'would betray the Republic' and reporting back to Stack.

29   Ibid., J.M. Maxwell to B.J. Goff, 6 February 1922. Goff was a solicitor who acted as a temporary Circuit Judge and was later appointed a District Justice.

30   Ibid., Report to Government Ministry, 29 August 1922, a lengthy disclosure of the subversive and political tendencies of staff members, most of whom were no longer with the department. Crump, who wrote it, seemed to have relished his role as spy!

31   Ibid., Browne to Duggan, 22 March 1922.

32   NA, DE 1/4 Minutes of Meeting Dáil Cabinet, 24 February 1922.

33   NA, Minutes of Provisional Government, G.1., Vol 1, 8 March 1922.

34 UCD Archives, Kennedy Papers, P4/1067.

35 NA, D/Jus, H140/1, Duggan to Browne, 25 March 1922.

36 A small staff under Sir James McMahon was retained at Dublin Castle until the end of 1922.

37 NA, CSO, R9/1-10.

38 NA, CSO, R 10/1, letters from Resident Magistrates between 15 February and 26 March 1922.

39 Although both the Government of Ireland Act 1920 and the Treaty provided for voluntary retirement of Resident Magistrates, it became clear during post-Treaty negotiations that they were not to be given a choice. In July and August 1922 Kennedy was taking soundings about the level of pensions, but the public announcement came only at the last minute: it was greeted with almost universal approval. J.A. Costello wrote a memorandum on their origins and powers, 6 September 1922, possibly in preparation for the appointment of District Justices. UCD Archives, Kennedy Papers, P4/1067.

40 NA, CSO, R 10/1, Herries-Crosbie to Under Secretary, 26 March 1922.

41 Ibid., C.H. Robinson to Under Secretary, 1 March 1922.

42 *Limerick Weekly Echo*, 4 February 1922.

43 *The Kerry People* reported that they had protested 'against a military ukase issued by people who had appointed themselves', 29 April 1922. It appeared that duly appointed judges could not win; already their courts were being spoken of with nostalgia. The proceedings of the Republican District Court in Nenagh were described as reminiscent 'of the old Quarter Sessions or Assizes ... utmost decorum within and without the building' (*King's County Chronicle*, 23 February 1922).

44 Such definitions were more likely to be uttered by judicial persons or solicitors in the earlier months than by government spokesmen, but by mid-July 1922 it was loudly trumpeted as official truth.

45 NA, DE 6/985-1287, which are the Dublin Corporation cases dealt with by the Winding-up Commission.

46 *Limerick Weekly Echo*, 8 April 1922.

47 Meredith was the first judge to summon a jury, NA, DE 11/147.

48 NA, DE 26/6.

49 NA, DE 27/1, 3 June 1922: it was rather late to be issuing instructions when juries had been a regular feature for two months.

50 *King's County Chronicle*, 30 March 1922.

51 *The Irish Times*, 15 April 1922. The group of Republican officers under Rory O'Connor who set up headquarters in the Four Courts on 13 April 1922 gave interviews and issued statements to the press.

52 'Lord Chief Justice wrote regarding arrangements he proposed to make in order to carry on business of Courts interrupted by occupation of the Four Courts'. NA, G.1., Vol. 1, Minutes of Provisional Government, 18 April 1922.

53 J. Bowyer Bell, *The Secret Army: The IRA 1916–1979* (Dublin, 1979), pp. 29–34.

Chapter 6

1   NA, DE 25/5 Report of Ministry for Home Affairs (MHA), April Session 1922. Under Police Department, details were given of a challenge contained in a letter which Simon Donnelly wrote to the Adjutant General, 27 March 1922, to the effect that he was awaiting dismissal since he had attended the Army Convention the previous day: on being dismissed, he removed books, papers, and typewriters from Headquarters, Brunswick Street. When Captain Ennis, who was appointed to take over, arrived there on 30 March, he found that all the staff, two typists and three clerks had also left.

2   NA, DE 13/3 District Registrar, West Cavan was arrested for being in charge of a raid on Ballyduff Barracks: local justices were seeking permission to appoint a temporary registrar in his absence. Ennis, Chief of Police, to MHA 15 July 1922.

3   Conor Brady, *Guardians of the Peace* (Dublin, 1974), pp. 37–51; a comprehensive history of the Garda Síochána, or Civic Guards, in which the uncertain first steps in their establishment are particularly examined.

4   NA, DE 10/39, Padraic Ó Caoirinn, Parish Clerk, Carrickderry, to MHA, 11 February 1922.

5   Davitt, p. 81. His recollection was that the incident had taken place in Cahirciveen, Co. Kerry, sometime in March 1922.

6   Ibid, p. 80.

7   NA, DE 10/38 McNeice, Registrar, Limerick City, to Duggan, 31 July 1922.

8   W. N. Osborough, 'Law in Ireland 1916–26', *Northern Ireland Legal Quarterly*, Vol. 23, No. 1, 1972, pp. 56–7.

9   *Clonmel Chronicle*, 25 February 1922.

10 The justices of a parish court in north Tipperary resigned when the local IRA commander tried to intimidate them by claiming the courts were answerable to the IRA: the matter was the subject of a memorandum from General Headquarters on the necessity of keeping the civil administration separate from the military. NA, DE 10/ 59. Davitt also noted that the effect on the District Justices with whom he was sitting of the arrival of a woman litigant in the company of some members of the local Flying Column was the opposite of the one intended. She was a noted horsewoman, but he felt it was fortunate for her that the matter in dispute had been settled before the hearing. Davitt, p. 65.

11 NA, DE 13/3, Police Report to MHA.

12 The Dáil elected on that day did not convene until 9 September following.

13 NA, G. 1.2. Minutes of the Provisional Government, Vol. 2, 5 June 1922. Under the heading 'Summer Assizes', there was a decision that the Judges were to go out on circuit on 8 July and on 23 July Kennedy was authorised to issue their commissions. He appears to have prepared at least three different drafts in an effort to play down the central place of the King in the standard commission to Assize Judges, UCD Archives, Kennedy Papers, P.4/1067.

14 The bombardment of the Four Courts was followed by a week of intense fighting in Dublin and the outbreak of the Civil War.

15 The dates were 10, 12, 14, 19, 22, 24 and 26 July 1922. Minutes of Provisional Government, Vol. 2.

16 Ibid., 10 July 1922; it was the first discussion on the Dáil Courts since 8 March.

17 *The Irish Times*, 22 June 1922.

18 On the contrary, as late as 11 July Meredith and Davitt were informed by letter from Cleary, Registrar of the Supreme Court, of the cases listed for courts on the 13th, NA, DE 11/141 and 11/242.

19 NA, D/Jus, H 140/1. Correspondence files relating to Dáil Court matters.

20 NA, D/ Jus, H140/1. Nicholls to Duggan, Minister for Home Affairs, 11 July 1922.

21 When there was a query about his future deployment, the Secretary to Government wrote to Kennedy, pointing out that Nicholls had a definite status in the Provisional Government since he was to be in charge in the Minister's absence. Secretary to Kennedy, 29 September 1922, Kennedy Papers, P4/1067.

22 The text of the letter was given in newspaper reports, but there is no copy in Meredith's or Davitt's files with the records. However, there is a carbon copy of a letter dated 13 July 1922 to all District Registrars, informing them that the Dáil Éireann cabinet had ordered the cessation of Circuit Courts and they were to see that no further sittings were to be held pending reorganisation. The names of the four judges are pencilled in, with 'Kindly note the contents' added. The original notice signed by Nicholls is with the State file relating to the abolition of the Dáil Courts and also a handwritten communication from Nicholls saying that he had deliberately left it vague so that the judges could finish the current circuit if they wanted: however, he thought that they had been abandoned, but it was impossible to get news from the country, NA, D/T.S.1.449.

23 The Irish Bar met 'to consider the unsatisfactory position', *The Irish Times*, 14 July 1922.

24 NA, DE 13/5. The case was *Irish Kinematography Co. (1920)* v. *O'Connor and Bailey*. See also DE 12/39.

25 Davitt, pp. 90–5.

26 NA, D/Jus H140/1, Nicholls to Duggan, 11 July 1922. A telegram was sent to Meredith in Carlow but he had returned in the meantime.

27 DE 27/1, 13 July 1922. Also see Brian Farrell, 'The Legislation of a "Revolutionary" Assembly: Dáil Decrees, 1919–1922' (1975) 10 *Irish Jurist* (n.s.) 112, where he traces the steps taken by the Provisional Government towards the closing down of the courts before 25 July 1922.

28 George Noble Plunkett, hereditary papal count, was father of Joseph Mary Plunkett, executed in 1916, and of George, taken prisoner after the capture of the Four Courts. Count Plunkett was Minister for Foreign Affairs, later for Fine Arts in the Dáil government. He opposed the Treaty, and was Sinn Féin TD for County Roscommon, 1922–7.

29 A copy of the affadavit drafted by Michael Comyn KC was sent to Kennedy, who was asked if it might be a basis to prosecute Comyn for subornation of perjury and seditious libel. Kennedy hastened to advise that legal counsel were traditionally protected in law if they were following their client's legitimate instructions. UCD Archives, Kennedy Papers, P4/253 and P4/1070. Crowley later asserted that de

Valera wanted to use the occasion of Plunkett's application to test the legal validity of the Treaty. Whereas the affadavit did set out arguments about the integrity of the Republic, which were the common coinage of those who opposed the Provisional Government, it is hard to see how any decision of Crowley's could influence either side in the civil war already under way.

30　Dorothy Macardle, op. cit., p. 685.

31　NA, DE 34/70, *in re Morris* and 34/51, *in re Lawlor.*

32　NA, DE 34/70, *in re Morris*, Cleary, Register to Commandant. General O'Connor, 27 June 1922.

33　In its essentials, the same procedure applies today where a prisoner challenges the legality of his detention: application can be made to any judge of the High Court, Article 40.4.2. of the Constitution. A few days later, when Nicholls enquired about paying the judges' salaries, it was pointed out that no order of dismissal had been made. UCD Archives, Kennedy Papers, P4/1070, and the next chapter.

34　NA, DE 12/198, Meredith to Duggan, 24 July 1922.

35　NA, D/T, G.1.1, Minutes of Provisional Government, 25 July 1922.

36　Diarmuid Ó Cruadhlaoich (Crowley), *Step by Step: From the Republic Back into Empire The Evolution of Eamonn* [*sic*] *de Valera,* n.d., p. 6.

37　UCD Archives, Kennedy Papers, P4/252 – Censorship had been introduced on 28 June 1922.

38　'The attention of the Commander-in-Chief should be drawn to the matter'. NA, Minutes of Provisional Government, 2 August 1922.

39　*Iris Oifigiúil,* No.55, 1 August 1922, and it already had appeared in the public press on 28 July.

40　This lacuna was noted by Michael McDunphy, Assistant Secretary to the Government, in a memorandum he drafted the following day, in which he listed the events leading to the abolition of the courts and regarding the circumstances in which the Decree was issued, 'there is no record of any decisions by Cabinet of D.E. subsequent to 28th April 1922'. He observed that most of the members of the latter were the same persons who formed the Provisional Government and those that were not took part in its deliberations and therefore 'it is in essence correct to state that the Decree referred to was in fact issued with the concurrence of the Cabinet of Dáil Éireann but, as already stated, there is no record of any separate decision of Dáil Cabinet authorising the issue of the Decree by the Minister'. NA, T/D, S.1 449. Also, for a clear summary of the relation of the two cabinets in the context of the closure of the courts, see Farrell, 'The Legislation of a "Revolutionary" Assembly: Dáil Decrees, 1919–1922', (1975) 10 *Irish Jurist* (n.s.) 120–3.

41　The Dáil was twice prorogued and did not meet until 9 September 1922.

42　'The actual Constitution of the Courts was effected by the Minister for Home Affairs, and was, moreover, stated to be provisional. He could, presumably, have scrapped the provisional constitution and replaced it with another. He had, therefore, the power to abolish the Courts in the circumstances.' Davitt, p. 35. However, it is possible to argue that a minister who is responsible for setting up a body or regulations to put into effect the provisions of any Act of Parliament is not thereby considered to be given the power to repeal the Act itself. More importantly, Davitt seems to have overlooked the fact that the Minster did not claim such power: he purported to be carrying out a decision of the Dáil Éireann cabinet.

43 The Dublin Metropolitan Police Force – the DMP – was not part of the Royal Irish Constabulary: it continued as a separate force until it was merged with the Garda Síochána in 1925, Brady, op. cit., pp. 131–3.

44 *The Irish Times*, 14 July 1922. Draft of official statement dated 13 July is with Kennedy Papers, P4/1068.

45 Blythe and Kennedy appear to be the only sources for the 'illegality' of the Dáil Courts. Davitt never refers to it and O'Higgins forebore to add it to the list of shortcomings in the Dáil Debate on the Winding-up Bill a year later.

46 Blythe's appointment took effect from 18 July 1922: however, although not a member of either the Provisional or the Dáil cabinet, he had been attending government meetings since May 1922, NA, D/T, Minutes of the Provisional Government, Vol. 2, 18 July 1922.

47 Copies of the memorandum are with the Blythe, Kennedy and Mulcahy Papers, UCD Archives; it has no date but was written between the suspension of the superior courts and 25 July 1922; Blythe Papers P24/72.

48 Kennedy Papers, UCD Archives, P4/1067.

49 *R. (Kelly)* v. *Maguire and O'Shiel and others* (1923), 2 IR 58. The plaintiff had brought prohibition proceedings against a Dáil Land Court decision on the division of his lands; the High Court held that it could neither take judicial notice of nor issue a writ of prohibition to an illegal body.

50 'The petitioners having miscalculated their remedy, we do not give them costs; we do not grant costs against them', Dodd, J., *ibid.*

51 He later called it 'a desperate act of official lawlessness' in a leaflet in August 1923 (in the possession of his son, Mr Colm Gavan Duffy).

52 UCD Archives, Kennedy Papers, copy letter Vignoles, Court Organiser to MHA, 27 July 1922; he suggested that District and Circuit Courts be organised with professional judges assisted by lay representatives chosen by the people.

53 Liam Sweeney, the Donegal Registrar with the vivid turn of phrase, wrote: 'In the [*Irish*] *Independent* on Friday I read that the Republican Courts are to cease to function and that the courts (which we were taught to call enemy courts) are to carry on. … We were directed to do all in our power to upset the working of the (British) Courts and now when we have done so; when British Courts are a dead letter they are resurrected and we are ordered quietly to give way to them. … We established our courts so well that no place in the constituency have the British Courts for months. …

It may be alright to say all courts in Ireland are now Irish Courts but you cannot make a lion into a mouse by naming him one and the men who rule and work these (Irish) Courts are the men who support England as loyally as any Black and Tan could do: now England has deserted them the Free State is going to befriend themthem. … We are not responsible for foisting this part of England's left luggage on the backs of the Irish people; whoever is will merit few supporters.' Sweeney to Minister, 16 July 1922, NA, DE 11/20.

54   Nicholls, in his report of 27 February 1922, had recommended the appointment of legally qualified judges.

55   UCD Archives, Kennedy Papers, P4/1078, Kennedy to Joseph Gleeson, Solicitor, 5 August 1922.

56   UCD Archives, Mulcahy Papers, P 7/B/29 (1922) Collins to Provisional Government, 25 July 1922.

57   NA, DE 12/487.

58   This small force had been recruited by Collins and had its headquarters at Oriel House, Westland Row, Dublin, Brady, op.cit., pp. 31–6.

59   A Mr Tobin of the *Freeman's Journal* furnished Kennedy with first-hand account of the court sitting. UCD Archives, Kennedy Papers, P4/253: a typed copy of Tobin's statement is with the file in the National Archives, D/T, S.1.449. also in DE 9/13.

60   Peter Ennis, Police Chief, reported to MHA and Cleary was instantly dismissed. NA, D/Jus H140/1.

61   A report was sent by the Government Ministry for Home Affairs to the Commander in Chief and the Adjutant General warning of Mr Noyk's unsuitability to be given legal work by the Army, NA, D/Jus, H140/4, 2 September 1922.

62   *Davitt Memoir*, p. 106, where Crowley's letter to Gavan Duffy, whose assistance he invoked, is reproduced; Gavan Duffy later claimed that it had not reached him. Crowley had sent Davitt a copy.

63   'Mr Davitt is the best man for Judge Advocate General. The appointment is of utmost importance and the position must be taken up without delay'. Kennedy's memorandum to Minister, 7 August 1922. UCD Archives, Kennedy Papers, P4/258.

64   NA, D/Jus, H140/8, Army Finance Office to Secretary, Ministry of Home Affairs, 5 June 1923.

65   Gavan Duffy warned that arbitrary arrest was the most dangerous power in the hands of the Executive, and while he understood Judge Crowley as a cantankerous and difficult person, it was still wrong to imprison him and other people without a trial. Crowley had just been released and when Cosgrave was asked why he had been let out, he replied, 'Because he was an old cod. And I think that Deputy Gavan Duffy himself informed me one time that that was his real title of distinction'. Dáil Debates, Vol. 1 cols. 288–9, 14 September 1922.

Chapter 7

1   Simply put, the Provisional Government was to take over the functions of the administration of Southern Ireland or the twenty-six counties, heretofore under imperial control, but only until such time as a general election could be held. The primary purpose of the parliament then elected would be the approval of a constitution for the Irish Free State. The establishment of the State and the enactment of the Constitution would coincide. For the British view, see Lionel Curtis' Memorandum to Churchill, 24 May 1922: 'A further difficulty ... informal elections are to produce a constituent assembly which from our point of view has

no legislative power. This constituent assembly is to discuss the constitution.' PRO, CO 739.6.

2   Dáil Debates, Vol. 1, 9 September 1922, c. 56. Cosgrave had prefaced his remarks by saying that both governments had been coalesced for three or four months, and that they had met in common under a single chairman. The statement has little meaning: it is unlikely that the President intended to air-brush Griffith so rapidly from recent history. He was only a few weeks dead and he had been elected by Dáil Éireann as its President.

3   Dáil Debates, 30 November 1922, cols 2472- 4.

4   NA, G.1., Vol 3, Minutes of Provisional Government, 4 October 1922. Although Arthur Clery is named to be on the Committee, he did not participate.

5   NA DE 12/198, memorandum signed by Meredith and additional memorandum dated August 1922.

6   Ibid., Judicature (Transitory Provisions) Decree, 1922.

7   Ibid., O'Friel to Kennedy, 3 October 1922.

8   UCD Archives, Kennedy Papers, P4/1067.

9   The Dáil Decree had given responsibility for setting up the courts to the Minister for Home Affairs; the Land Courts remained solely under the authority of the Minister for Agriculture.

10   *The Judiciary*, p. 30.

11   UCD Archives, Kennedy Papers, P4/1068, Meredith to Kennedy, 14 October 1922.

12   UCD Archives, Kennedy Papers, P4/218, Order of King in Council, Windsor Castle, 1 March 1922.

13   It might have had echoes of the situation feared in a habeas corpus application to Crowley, 25 July 1922.

14   'And restrain their proceedings when they exceeded the jurisdiction which had been entrusted to them by the body which they professed to serve' and his conclusion: 'The answer is that this Court, while it prohibits and quashes the orders of inferior tribunals which exceed their jurisdiction, does not take notice of bodies which act openly and avowedly in defiance of the law. This Court has never issued a writ of prohibition or certiorari to an illegal body which challenges the authority of the Government and with which it is the duty of the Government to deal.' Moloney, L.C.J. in *The King (Kelly and others.)* v. *Conor Maguire and others* (1923) 57 ILTR.

15   Cf. Kennedy draft letter for Minister to send to Meredith and Davitt, stressing the 'illegality' of the Dáil Courts, UCD Archives, Kennedy Papers, P4/1067.

16   Prisoners who challenged custody were sometimes released for reasons of expediency. 'Frank Purcell arrested and detained in Lucan Barracks ... application for Habeas Corpus would probably be made. ... Should be released immediately.' NA, Provisional Government Minutes, 26 July 1922.

But when another prisoner, Frederick Quinn, serving a ten-year sentence imposed by the Recorder of Dublin, went on hunger strike in pursuit of a demand to have his case heard in a Republican Court, Kevin O'Shiel advised that it should not be conceded. 'It would be a most dangerous precedent ... would give criminal elements the impression we were half afraid of them.' O'Shiel Memorandum, 8 June 1922, NA, D/T, S.1. 238.

17 There was much juggling by officials – and sometimes politicians – to placate one side or the other, *Murphy* v. *Larkin,* NA, DE 12/325. In *Collins and Collins,* an appeal to the Registrar to delay proceedings in the High Court was mooted, DE 12/487, Sheehan to Kennedy, 23 April 1923, and arbitration between the parties was quietly arranged, UCD Archives, P4/557.

18 Brady, op.cit., pp. 71–88.

19 The term 'District Justice' neutralised possible opprobrium that they had actually been appointed as Resident Magistrates.

20 Notice that all the Dáil Courts had been brought to an end was published in *Iris Oifigiúil,* 30 October 1922.

21 Several of them were talented beyond legal proficiency: Dermot Gleeson, Limerick, was a noted historian and archaeologist, Kenneth Reddin, Dublin, was a playwright and novelist, as was Louis Walsh, Donegal; and Richard Johnson's play *The Evidence I Shall Give* was produced in the Abbey Theatre in 1964 when he was still presiding over the courts in Kerry.

22 The attacks on District Justices were referred to by the Minister for Home Affairs, NA, G.2. Minutes of Provisional Government, 22 November 1922. It was directed that they were to continue their duties as usual.

23 At the first sitting in Ennis, Justice Gleeson said they were the servants of the people and not their masters, and he paid tribute to the 'magnificent and gratuitous manner' in which Parish and District Justices had carried out their duties, *Clare Champion*, 18 November 1922. At the Wexford Court, Justice Fahy stressed that the justices came from the people and were akin to them in their feelings, hopes and wishes, that they were the people's servants 'in dispensing justice to all parties, irrespective of creed or class', *New Ross Journal*, 24 November 1922.

24 The days in which the court would sit at various venues in County Clare – District No. 16 – were given in a list headed 'Court of District Sessions', *Clare Champion,* 23 December 1922.

25 Letters written by solicitors on behalf of their clients during this period are with the Ministry's correspondence files. NA, DE 12/ 1-488.

26 UCD Archives, Kennedy Papers, P4/557.

27 During the Dáil Debate on the Winding-up Bill, O'Higgins admitted that there had been such interference with the legal process, Dáil Debates, 24 July 1923, col. 1310.

28 Henry O'Friel had been dismissed from the public service in 1918 when he refused to take an oath of loyalty under the provisions of the Defence of the Realm Act. He served as a Dáil judge and became the chairman of Dublin County Council. He was asked by Kevin O'Higgins to take the position of Secretary to the Ministry of Home Affairs, later to be the Department of Justice. He left the Department around 1930 to become Chairman of the Tariff Commission. (Conversation with his son, Seamus O'Friel, FRCSI, Dublin.)

29 *Collins* v. *Collins*, NA, DE 12/466.

30 NA, DE 12/487, O'Brien Moran to MHA, 31 March 1923.

31 NA, DE 12/198.

32 NA, DE 27/11. Meredith urged that 'publication should be constituted as it will create a very favourable feeling amongst people and will weaken the opposition', DE 12/198.

33 NA, H 140/17, T. Gordon Flanagan to Roche, 20 June 1923.

34 NA, DE 12/466, O'Friel to O'Brien Moran, 4 April 1923; he suggested the advisability of having his client John Collins's decree registered, presumably to deflect attention away from proceedings in the High Court and postpone matters until legislation had been passed.

35 NA DE 12/487, Draft Bill.

36 The Committee which reported in October 1922 had recommended that only cases which had been embarked upon should be adjudicated; those that had merely been entered for hearing should be discontinued.

37 It should be noted that the case of *The King (Kelly)* v. *Maguire and O'Shiel* was heard almost a year after the Treaty.

38 The first departmental name change was from Ministry for Home Affairs to the Department of Justice, which was considered to imply a more restrictive application than 'Home Affairs', which might conceivably include every aspect of civic concern. UCD Archives, Kennedy Papers, P4/539.

39 NA, DE 12/487, 19 April 1923.

40 Among other temporary commissions were those dealing with malicious injuries claims, placements in the civil service and County Court appeals.

41 Correspondence between Finance and Justice on expenses of Commission continued up to 1927, NA, D/Jus, H 140/27.

42 UCD Archives, Kennedy Papers, P4/1071 Matheson to Kennedy, 2 July 1923.

43 Most Acts which give rise to a possible cause of action will prescribe the time limits within which such proceedings must be commenced.

44 UCD Archives, Kennedy Papers, Matheson to Kennedy, 2 July 1922.

45 The Bill was introduced on 19 July 1923, c. 1088; debate began 24 July, Dáil Debates, cols. 1306–7.

46 Darrell Figgis, *Recollections of the Irish War* (London, 1927), pp. 294–300.

47 Tom Johnson's interventions in the debate brought a note of reassuring common sense, particularly given the aggressive atmosphere generated by O'Higgins's opposition to any suggested amendments.

48 Dáil Debates, Vol. 3, 24 July 1922, cols. 1307–8.

49 'When these Courts reappeared during the Truce period they were not as careful and not as pure in their administration as they were in their first youth and enthusiasm. They gave in many places, or purported to give, certificates to people to deal in intoxicating liquor. They had no such jurisdiction.' O'Higgins, Dáil Debates, 24 July 1922, col. 1307.

50 *The Judiciary* excluded lay judges from dealing with any such applications. 'Equity cases shall, except by direction of the Circuit Judge, be decided exclusively by the Circuit Judge, who may if he thinks fit refer the hearing of the case to himself or to a hearing of the Supreme Court in Dublin' (p. 6). Under 'definitions', equity cases include proceedings for injunctions (p. 8).

51   O'Higgins's irrascible and irrational attitude throughout the debate cannot be wholly explained by his general arrogance, nor was it directed solely at Gavan Duffy, whom he persisted in treating as a renegade because of his resignation from the Dáil cabinet on a point of principle. He refused to take Fitzgibbon's objections into account either. It may have been in part because they were experienced lawyers and he was only one by training, and not by profession. The Dáil Courts remained a sore point and the reasons for the sudden closure were never satsifactorily explained. Maurice Moynihan, who was a young civil servant in 1925, asked Michael Hayes about it and got an airy dismissal with a remark to the effect that there were people who thought all history had begun in 1916. He got the impression that it was a matter not to be pursued. Mr Moynihan told the author that his interest was because his brother, Seán Moynihan, later Secretary to the Department of Finance, had been a Dáil judge in Kerry. More than forty years later, Davitt's gentle comment was that O'Higgins's remarks had been 'somewhat ungracious'. 'The Civil Jurisdiction of the Dáil Courts' (1968) 3 *Irish Jurist*, 129.

52   Gerald Fitzgibbon was later among the first appointees to the Supreme Court in 1924.

53   While O'Higgins may have received private representations made to him by business interests, there are none in the files. On the contrary, many firms initiated proceedings in the Dáil courts, particularly in Dublin where there was a real alternative. Moreover, the provision extended relief to any person who as far back as 1916 had not even issued a writ for whatever reason.

54   NA, G2.1 Minutes of Executive Council, 26 July 1923.

55   Dáil Debates, Vol. 4, 31 July 1923, col. 1685.

56   Ibid., 30 July 1923, cols. 1665–6.

57   In the Bill, one could only proceed on foot of a registered decree when application had first been made to the Commissioners for consent.

58   NA, D/Jus, H 140/17 and DE 17/7. When Nicholls failed to get offices for the Dáil Ministry in Dublin Castle in January 1922, he was very aggrieved, H 140/1.

59   It had been the Mainguard House. Meredith's patronage of the arts in having paintings restored was noted in a newspaper article, cutting in NA, DE 1/1.

60   Meredith had been closely associated with the drafting of the legislation at all stages.

61   The Committee had recommended that as far as possible former judges should be appointed to avoid 'awkwardness and embarrassment'.

62   Kevin O'Shiel, a barrister from Northern Ireland, wrote a series of recollections in the *Irish Times*, November 1966. In 1922 he acted as Assistant Law Officer, and was later a Judicial Land Commissioner.

63   Conor Maguire had refused to give an account of his whereabouts at the start of the Civil War, as required from all civil servants: he pointed out that he was a judge, not a civil servant. He resigned or was suspended. When he was Attorney General in 1933, he applied for three months' arrears of salary, between July and September 1922. NA, D/T, S.1 315. At the time in question, early in July 1922, he

brought Erskine Childers to his own home to prevent Childers's arrest, Maguire to Frank Gallagher, 2 December 1959, NLI, Gallagher Papers, 21244.

64 Arthur Clery, Professor of Law, UCD, ignored the offer of a pension or judicial office, NA, O/Jus, H1140/8.

65 NA, O/T, S I 499, Crowley to de Valera, 3 October 1934, in which he said that because de Valera was in prison at the time, Patrick Ruttledge, as acting President and Minister for Home Affairs in the (Republican) Third Dáil, 'gave me a licence to act as a member of the Commission to try the cases that had been pending in the Republican Courts at the time those courts were suppressed'.

66 It was decided that the Commissioners would go out on circuit and deal with pending matters in the country, while the Registry caught up, O'Friel to Department of Finance, 29 October 1923, NA, D/Jus, H140/13.

67 For McQuaid's undistinguished career in the Commission, see author's M.Litt. thesis, 'The Origins, Establishment and Work of the Dáil Courts Winding-Up Commission', 1991, Trinity College, Dublin, pp. 101–43.

68 McQuaid's first Report, 13 November 1923, NA D/Jus, H140/22.

69 Alternatively, the Commissioners could have provided for an exemption under the Rules.

70 NA, H 140/25. O'Friel to O'Higgins, 24 August 1923.

71 Ibid., Kennedy to Coyne, Private Secretary to O'Higgins, 28 August 1923.

72 Ibid., Macauley to O'Higgins, 29 November 1923.

73 An order of certiorari is sought to stop a court exceeding its jurisdiction, e.g. by making an order which it has no power to do.

74 The cost of living bonus brought the salaries to about £1,726 and £1,448, respectively.

75 DE 1/1. The Collins case was the first listed for hearing by the Commissioners. For a fuller account, see author's thesis, Chapter 7, Part 2.

76 NA, DE 12/466 application by defendant (Matthew Collins) for leave to appeal against registration was dated August 1923, which was two months before he received notification that the decree, in fact, had been registered.

77 'As this is the first application for leave to appeal against the decision of the Dáil Supreme Court we have though it advisable to deliver a considered judgement ... so as to indicate ... considerations [which] should weigh with us in the exercise of our discretion'. Opening words of judgement, dated 7 November 1923 and signed by Meredith, NA, DE 34/23.

78 Ibid., pp. 11–12.

79 Ibid., p. 12.

80 Although the defendant had applied for an injunction to restrain John Collins from interference with the lands, it was not the kind of injunction to which Meredith was referring. The irony was that the only practical step taken in the Collins case to interfere in the function of another court was made by a government department when Sheehan, Home Affairs, asked Kennedy if the High Court Registrar might be persuaded to delay the proceedings there. Kennedy, prudently, forebore to give a

written reply until he was in a position to refer Sheehan to the remedy in the Act. NA, DE 12/466.

81 They hoped by the time they had completed what work there was outside Dublin, the Registry would have more cases ready for hearing.

82 T.G. Burke was Crowley's registrar. 'Dermot Crowley, while acting as a Commissioner to conclude the functions of the said Courts, appointed me to act as his Clerk while he was holding sittings to decide pending cases yet unheard.' Judge Burke in a handwritten statement to the author, Galway, February 1993. All the registrars were young barristers or pupils at the beginning of their careers. When Meredith urged that they be paid better allowances – so as not to be beholden to solicitors for hospitality – O'Friel thought the 'inducement was sufficient amounting to the certainty of a small brief every day for six weeks'. O'Friel to Meredith, 12 February 1924, NA, D/Jus, H 140/23.

83 *Limerick Leader*, 24 April 1924.

84 NA DE 37/3, Crowley to McQuaid, 14 November 1923.

85 Robert de Courcy brought in custody from the Curragh, *Limerick Leader*, 28 April 1924.

86 Crowley commented that solicitors in Limerick and Clare were quite unprepared and had not read the Rules – the air of *laissez-faire* was not confined to those counties, as is evident from solicitors' correspondence with Registrar, NA, DE 40, 1–5, 41.

87 All applications for registration had to be received by 25 October 1923.

88 NA, H 140/17, McQuaid to O'Friel, 11 September 1923.

89 NA, H 140/22, first Weekly Report, 13 November 1923.

90 NA, H 140/26 O'Friel to Meredith, 2 January 1924.

91 By November 1924, there appeared to be no prospect of finalising the work, and O'Friel had come to believe that the better course would be to hand it over to the High Court as 'ongoing'. Having come to this conclusion, it was easy enough to find justification in the nature of certain judgements that require to remain under court supervision.

92 The Commission could never have been wound up in the ordinary sense, a lesson that could have been learnt from the closing of the Dáil Courts. Once decrees were registered or appeals heard and decided, they became part of the *res judicata* – i.e., things decided and therefore enforceable and attracting judicial notice. Moreover, owing to Gavan Duffy's prescience, a Dáil Court decree could be cited in an action or raised as a defence for ever.

93 John O'Byrne, Attorney General, to Minister for Justice, 7 January 1925; NA, D/Jus, H140/I7.

94 Ibid.

95 Charles Stewart Kenny was the last Commissioner; he was not appointed Chief Judicial Commissioner, a serious oversight because such an appointment was legally essential to the operation of the Act.

96 A Commissioner had twice the salary of a Dáil Judge, plus security, expenses and public status, apart from the near certainty of permanent judicial office.

97   Crowley sued the State in 1934; the case is discussed in the next chapter.
98   Kenny was appointed to the District Court; Sheehy and Wyse Power became Circuit Judges.
99   For the transfer of the records to the High Court, see UCD Archives, Kennedy Papers, P4/1072.
100 *Clare Champion*, 1 August 1925.

Chapter 8

1   NA, D/T, G.1.2 Minutes of Provisional Government, 10 July 1922.
2   Brian Farrell, 'The Drafting of the Irish Constitution; III, (1971) 6 (ns) *Irish Jurist* pp. 130–2. Articles 38–43 in Draft B provided only in the most general terms for a Supreme Court and courts of first instance.
3   NA, D/T, G.1. 3 Minutes of Provisional Government, 12 September 1922.
4   The references to the proceedings of the Committee are to be found in UCD Archives, Kennedy Papers; although Michael Smithwick was Secretary to the Committee, its deliberations appears to have been coordinated by Kennedy.
5   UCD Archives, Kennedy Papers, Pa/1067, Meredith to Kennedy, 28 August 1922, when he suggested James Douglas, a Dublin businessman, who later became Vice-Chairman of Seanad Éireann.
6   UCD Archives, Kennedy Papers, P4/1090.
7   Ibid., P4/1067, Kennedy to McNeill, 29 August 1922.
8   Ibid., P4/1092. The section includes other letters and submissions addressed to the prospect of a new legal system.
9   Ibid.
10   Ibid., Johnson to Secretary, Judiciary Committee, 2 May 1923, forwarding 'certain views of the National Executive of the Irish Labour Party and Trade Union Congress upon the subject of the Committee's labours.'
11   NA, D/Jus, HA 140/8; also infra.
12   UCD Archives, Kennedy Papers, P4/1067, Walsh to Kennedy, 25 July 1922.
13   Ibid., B.J. Goff to Kennedy, 26 August 1922.
14   Ibid., Vignoles to Nicholls, 26 August 1922.
15   Hugh Kennedy became Attorney General after the passing of the Constitution, 6 December 1922.
16   UCD Archives, Kennedy Papers, P4/1092.
17   Ibid. Kennedy and Walsh were particularly agreed on the point; exchange of letters, 28 February and 7 March 1923.
18   The accompanying draft of the letter to be sent was signed by the Chairman of the Seanad and of the Committee 'Faithfully yours, Glenavy'; he left the address of his London club with Smithwick on 17 May 1923 in case any matter of urgency arose on the report. The President of the Executive Council was a bit more effusive in his reply: 'I am, Lord Glenavy, Your obedient servant.' UCD Archives, Kennedy Papers, P4/1095.

19   Ibid. P4/1097; 'I send you herewith a recopy of your draft Bill ...' Kennedy to
      Arthur C. Meredith, 7 July 1923.
20   Ibid., and previous chapter.
21   Ibid., P4/1098.
22   Ibid., P4/587 Cosgrave to Kennedy, July 1923 (before 22 July), listing Bills expected
      to pass uncontended before the end of the current session.
23   Dáil Debates, 31 July 1923, col. 1716.
24   Cosgrave speaking in Dáil, 31 August 1923. cols. 1215–6.
25   Dáil Debates, Vol. 5, 25 September 1923, cols. 84–5.
26   Ibid., 12 October 1923, c. 377.
27   Ibid., 1 October 1923, c. 387.
28   Ibid, 31 October 1923, c. 477.
29   Captain Redmond speaking in the Dáil, 11 October 1923, Dáil Debates, col. 284.
30   Ibid., col. 283.
31   The amendment would have fixed the retirement age for District Justices at seventy
      rather than sixty-five. Dáil Debates, 31 October 1923, col. 498.
32   Dáil Debates, 11 November 1923, col. 583.
33   Ibid., col. 579.
34   Had his proposal been adopted, it would have provided the kind of pre-trial
      hearing designed to encourage conciliation, which, in one form or another, is a
      feature of many legal systems the world over, although not in Ireland, Cappelletti
      and Garth, *Access to Justice,* 4 vols. Milan, 1978–9.
35   Seanad Debates, 16 January 1924, col. 411.
36   Kennedy filed the cutting, UCD Archives, Kennedy Papers, P4/1094.
37   Seanad Debates, 25 January 1924, col. 616.
38   Ibid., cols. 533–4.
39   Dáil Debates, 31 October 1923, col. 583.
40   Seanad Debates, 6 March 1924, col. 1134.
41   Ibid., col. 1128.
42   Courts Act, 1991, S.21, ss I (a) and (b).
43   Ibid., 3 April 1924, col. 1314.
44   Seanad Debates, 16 January 1924, cols. 614–5.
45   Cosgrave's response to the debate in Dáil and Seanad appears to be out of character.
      For an assessment of Cosgrave as President of the Executive Council, see Brian Farrell,
      Chairman or Chief? Dublin, 1971, pp. 18–25. His rather hysterical performance at
      this time may have been due to the toll of the Civil War and the burden of office on
      his physical and mental health. Nevertheless, he seriously miscalculated the strong
      feelings of deputies and senators about the constitution of a new judicial system.
      Kennedy privately agreed with them: 'You may take it that everything that savours in
      the very least of the old R.M.s and the pollution of justice by Castle interference will
      be opposed tooth and nail and indeed, I, personally, will not stand for anything of the
      kind'. Kennedy to Department of Finance, UCD Archives, Kennedy Papers, P4/724.
46   'The result is that in one generation you will have no learned Bar, you will have no
      learned Bench, and if you have no learned Bench, you will have no real protection

for the poor and weak in this Country. Senator Brown, speaking on behalf of the Law Society and the Provisional Solicitors' Association, when he urged that the limit of Circuit Court jurisdiction should be reduced from £300 to £100, Seanad Debates, 7 January 1924, cols. 721–2.

47 Adaption of Enactments Act 1922, Section 6.

48 Liam Coyne (Liam Ua Cadhain), *The Law Courts in Eire*, n.d., p. 46. (The author is grateful to Mr Padraig Ó'Murchu for bringing this book to her notice. He bought it in 1942 in preparation for an interview for a position in the District Court Service, in which he rose to be the Chief Examiner.)

49 District Justices (Temporary Provisions) Act 1923.

50 *Clare Champion*, 18 November, and *New Ross Journal*, 24 November 1923.

51 Among them were Richard Johnson (Kerry), Kenneth Reddin (Dublin), and Dermot Gleeson (Limerick).

52 'Digest of Criminal and Quasi Criminal Law from the year 1914' written as a supplement to *The Irish Justice of the Peace*, edited by George Gavan Duffy, Dublin 1925.

53 NA, D/Jus H140/8 Sheehan to Secretary, Department of Finance, 10 September 1923.

54 Ibid., Gregg to O'Friel, 24 September 1923.

55 Ibid., Memorandum, approved by O'Higgins, 4 February 1924.

56 Ibid.

57 Ibid., O'Byrne to O'Friel, 23 August 1923.

58 UCD Archives, Kennedy Papers, Letter Drafted by Kennedy for Minister for Home Affairs to send to Meredith and Davitt, draft dated 22 July 1922. P4/1067. See also previous chapter.

59 NA, D/Jus, H140, Crowley to O'Friel, 1 July 1924.

60 Dáil Supreme Court (Pensions) Act 1925.

61 NA, O/Jus, H140/8, Roche to Minister for Justice, 22 April 1932.

62 Ibid., Plenary Summons No. 70 of 1934, Ó Cruadhlaoich and Minister for Justice and Minister for Finance, Saorstát Éireann.

63 *Ó Cruadhlaoich v. Minister for Finance* (1934) 68 ILTR. 174.

64 N.L.I., C.O. P.100. The author is described as 'Judge of the Supreme Court of the Irish Republic' and the publication is undated. In 1964, it was serialised in *United Irishman*.

65 There is a list of court personnel in NA, DE 38/I n.d. with remarks and recommendations written against some names. Mr Ó Murchu, former Examiner of the District Court, was good enough to go through the list with the author and he recognised several names as men who had been clerks in the District Court when he began working there in 1942.

66 NA. D/Jus, H 140/29. It was acknowledged with thanks. The cheque book is in the possession of Mrs Ann McDonagh, daughter of the late Mrs Herron. An early childhood memory shared with her siblings is of police coming to arrest her mother because of her association with the Dáil Court.

67 NA, D/T S.1.449.

68　There is a copy of the Minutes in the Sinn Féin Funds Case file, Book 27, in the National Archives.

69　Liam Coyne, *The Law Courts of Eire*, Dublin, n.d.

70　UCD Archives, Kennedy Papers, P4/1067. Molony to Kennedy, 15 July 1922, 'as we may expect some additional business in consequences of the suspension of the sittings of the Republican Courts.'

71　PRO, CO. 739.6. The sub-committee to consider the position of persons holding judicial office in Ireland comprised Sir Claud Schuster, Permanent Secretary to the British Lord Chancellor, and Messrs Short and Antrobus of the Home Office, among others; there had been meetings on 23 June and 6 July. The Irish contingent who attended on the later date said that none of the Irish judges would accept service in the Free State if it were to be considered that the imperial obligation to them was thereby discharged. They also wanted a tribunal of the Lord Chief Justice and the Master of the Rolls in England and the Northern Irish Chief Justice to decide on terms of service offered by the Irish State.

72　Ibid. 'None of this will materialise until the judges have been offered and accepted office under the Free State. There are three contingencies: the Free State may not offer them a judicial appointment or may not offer them the same appointment. [Terms might be refused, bargains broken or positions, if accepted, made intolerable.] It seems reasonable that they should fix a contingent liability but here again we would only do so after negotiations with the Free State.' Schuster to Antrobus, 15 July 1922.

73　Courts of Justice Act 1924, which took effect in two stages.

74　*The Freeman's Journal*, 11 June 1924.

75　*The Irish Times*, 11 June 1924.

76　'As one of the judges of the Irish Free State I desire to express to you the satisfaction I feel at the momentous change that has taken place in the destiny of our country and convey my respectful congratulations on your appointment as Minister for Home Affairs. I cordially and undeservedly tender to the President and yourself my services for any particular purposes for which they may be required in the great work of transferring and reconstruction that now lies in your hands'. W.J. Johnston to Duggan, 16 January 1922, NA, DE 11/90.

77　Leon O'Broin, *W.E. Wylie and the Irish Revolution 1916–1921* (Dublin, 1989), pp. 27–9.

78　Ibid., pp. 23–4.

79　*The Freeman's Journal*, 12 June 1924.

80　*The Irish Times*, 12 June 1924.

81　UCD Archives, Kennedy Papers, P4/1054 (25). W.H. Dodd to Kennedy, 12 June 1924.

82　*In re the Solicitors (Ireland) Act 1898 and Sir James O'Connor* [1930] IR 623, 64 I.L.T.R. 25.

83　UCD Archives, Kennedy Papers, P4/1058 (40), Fitzgerald-Kenney to Kennedy.

84　Ibid., P4/1055.

85　Ronan Fanning, *Independent Ireland*, Dublin, 1983, p. 67.

86 NA, D/T, S 1 449, Nicholls to Ministry of Home Affairs, Merrion Street, 5 September 1922.

87 Conversation with Ann McDonagh and Lorean Heron, daughter and son of the late Mrs Heron.

89 The author, who was a solicitor's apprentice at the time, still remembers the frisson of excitement at such daring.

Bibliography

Unpublished Sources

National Archives
Records of Dáil Éireann Courts Commission
Documents in Sinn Féin Funds Case
Chief Secretary of Ireland's papers
Department of An Taoiseach files
Ministry of Home Affairs and Department of Justice files
Robert Barton papers

National Library of Ireland
Stack papers
Kent papers
Gallagher papers

Archives, University College, Dublin
Kennedy papers
Blythe papers
McGilligan papers
Mulcahy papers

Public Record Office, Kew
Cabinet papers
Home Office and Colonial Office papers
Papers of the Irish Affairs Committee
Memoir of Mr Justice Cahir Davitt in the possession of Mr Kevin Haugh, S.C.
Papers of Mr Justice Gavan Duffy in the possession of Mr Colm Gavan Duffy

Periodicals, Pamphlets, Newspapers

Dáil Debates and Seanad Debates
Irish Law Times and Solicitors' Journal
Iris Oifigiúil
Law Society Gazette
Irish Jurist
Capuchin Annual

Political Pamphlets, O'Brien Gift, NLI
Ó Cruadhlaoich, *Step by Step*, NLI

The Freeman's Journal
The Irish Times
Irish Independent
Limerick Leader
Limerick Weekly Echo
The Clare Champion
Tipperary People
Belfast Newsletter
New Ross Journal
Western News
Kerry People
King's County Chronicle

General Bibliography

Andrews, C.S., *Dublin Made Me*, Dublin, 1979.
—, *Man of No Property*, Cork, 1982.
Beckett, J.C., *The Making of Modern Ireland, 1603–1923*, London, 1966.
Bowman, John, *De Valera and the Ulster Question 1917–1973*, Oxford, 1982.
Bowyer Bell, J., *The Secret Army: The IRA 1915–1979*, Dublin, 1979.
Boyce, D. George, *English Men and Irish Troubles: British Public Opinion and the Making of Irish Policy*, London, 1972.
Boyle, Andrew, *The Riddle of Erskine Childers*, London, 1977.
Brady, Conor, *Guardians of the Peace*, Dublin, 1974.

Brennan, Robert, *Allegiance*, Dublin, 1950.

Broeker, J., *Rural Disorder and Police Reform in Ireland 1812–36*, London, 1970.

Cardozo, Nancy, *Maud Gonne*, London, 1979.

Casey, James, *The Office of the Attorney General in Ireland*, Dublin, 1980.

Churchill, W.S., *The World Crisis: The Aftermath*, London, 1929.

Colum, Padraic, *Arthur Griffith*, Dublin, 1959.

Coogan, T.P., *Michael Collins*, London, 1990.

Corran, J.M., *The Birth of the Irish Free State, 1921–3*, Alabama, 1980.

Coyne, Liam, *The Law Courts in Eire*, Dublin, n.d.

Davis, Richard, *Arthur Griffith and Non-violent Sinn Féin*, Dublin, 1974.

Fanning, Ronan, *The Irish Department of Finance 1922–58*, Dublin, 1978.

—, *Independent Ireland*, Dublin, 1983.

Farrell, Brian, *The Founding of Dáil Eireann: Parliament and Nation-Building*, Dublin, 1971.

—, *Chairman or Chief?*, Dublin, 1971.

Figgis, Darrell, *Recollections of the Irish War*, London, 1927.

Fitzpatrick, David, *Politics and Irish Life, 1913–1921*, Dublin, 1977.

Foster, R.F., *Modern Ireland, 1600–1972*, London, 1988.

Gallagher, Frank (David Hogan), *The Four Glorious Years*, Dublin, 1953.

Garvin, Tom, *The Evolution of Irish Nationalist Politics*, Oxford, 1981.

—, *Nationalist Revolutionaries in Ireland 1858–1928*, Oxford, 1987.

Gaughan, J Anthony, *Austin Stack: Portrait of a Separatist*, Tralee, 1977.

Golding, G.M., *George Gavan Duffy 1882–1951*, Dublin, 1982.

Harkness, D.W., *The Restless Dominion: The Irish Free State in the British Commonwealth of Nations, 1921–31*, London, 1972.

Hopkinson, Michael, *Green against Green*, Dublin, 1988.

Jones, Thomas, *Whitehall Diary*. Vol. III: *Ireland 1918–1925*, edited by K. Middlemas, London, 1971.

Kee, Robert, *The Green Flag*, London, 1972.

Lawlor, Sheila, *Britain and Ireland, 1914–1923*, Dublin, 1983.

Lee, Joseph, *Ireland 1912–1985*, Cambridge, 1989.

Lyons, F.S.L., *Ireland Since the Famine*, London, 1971.

Macardle, Dorothy, *The Irish Republic* (Corgi edition), London, 1968.

Mansergh, Nicholas, *The Irish Question, 1840–1921*, London, 1973.

McColgan, John, *British Policy and the Irish Administration 1920–1922*, London, 1983.

Moloney, J. Charles, *The Riddle of the Irish*, London, 1927.

O'Broin, Leon, *No Man's Man*, Dublin, 1982.

—, *Just Like Yesterday*, Dublin, 1986.

—, Leon, *WE. Wylie and the Irish Revolution 1916–1921*, Dublin, 1989.

O'Connor, James, *History of Ireland 1798–1924*, London, 1925.

O'Malley, Ernie, *On Another Man's Wound*, Tralee, 1979.

—, *The Singing Flame*, Dublin, 1978.

Pakenham, Frank, *Peace by Ordeal*, London, 1937.

Sexton, Brendan, *Ireland and the Crown*, Dublin, 1989.

Taylor, Rex, *Michael Collins*, London, 1958.

Tierney, Michael, *Eoin McNeill*, Oxford, 1980.

Townshend, Charles, *The British Campaign in Ireland 1919–1921*, Oxford, 1975.

—, *Political Violence in Ireland*, Oxford, 1983.

White, Terence de Vere, *Kevin O'Higgins*, London, 1949.

Younger, Calton, *Ireland's Civil War*, London, 1968.

Index